NAVIGATING THE
LIPSTICK
JUNGLE

Go from Plain Jane to Getting What You Want, Need, & Deserve!

Other Books by Jane Hight McMurry

The Dance Steps of Life
The Etiquette Advantage
Etiquette for The Christ School Gentleman
Readers Theatre for Senior Citizens
Success is a Team Effort

NAVIGATING THE
LIPSTICK
JUNGLE

Go from Plain Jane to Getting What You Want, Need, & Deserve!

Jane Hight McMurry

Stellar Publishing

FIRST EDITION 2012

Library of Congress Cataloging-in-Publication Data

McMurry, Jane Hight.

Navigating the Lipstick Jungle: Go from Plain Jane to Getting What You Want, Need, and Deserve/Jane Hight McMurry.

Includes bibliographical references and index.

ISBN 0970304186

1. Business
2. Women

Library of Congress Control Number: 2011905695 (alk.paper)

Summary: A woman's guide to interpersonal skills for business and personal success.

Printed in the United States of America

10 9 8 7 6 5 4 3 2 1

Book design by Patricia Rasch

In thanksgiving and memory of my mother,
Joan Williams Hight

For my daughters,
Winifred Joan and Allison Louise

And for
Every Woman
who wants knowledge
beyond education and technical skills
to go from Plain Jane to getting what she
wants, needs, and deserves.

Acknowledgements

Prince Charming brings security to Cinderella in a fairy tale. My parents, Joan Williams and Henry Wesley Hight, Sr, brought security to me as a child. I frequently reference my mother in this book because it is for and about women. However, many of the life lessons I share in this book were learned from both of my parents and the opportunities they afforded me. I am forever grateful for their devoted commitment as parents who served as models of integrity and taught by example the importance of standing up for what is right even when it means standing alone.

The closing words of this book quote my mother's words to me about the gift of daughters, but I am equally sure that she felt that her son was one of her greatest gifts. I thank my brother, Chip, not only for being a sublime brother, but for being a shining example of a man of integrity. I thank male models of integrity—especially my father and my brother who value and respect women.

Special thanks to Belinda Landis who edited this work and to Steve Bentson, Katherine Christophe, Judy and RV Fulk, Patricia Koonce, Barbara Hight, and Linda and Warren McMurry.

Table of Contents

Chapter One

Getting What You Want in the Jungle

"Where are you going?" asked the Cheshire Cat.
"I don't know," Alice replied.
"Then any road will take you there," hissed the cat.

—*Alice in Wonderland*

Dear Women,

It's a jungle in the business world. If you want to survive and to capture the prey you want in the business world, you have to know what you need to do to achieve the results you want. Think about this: if you were going on safari into the deepest darkest jungles in Africa, would you just hop on a plane and go without thinking about the type of safari you're going on—the animals, their habitat, and the gear you need to be prepared? If you are not smart and don't have a good guide, you'll be eaten alive.

Prince Charming brings security to Cinderella in a fairy tale. In the real world, you must take control of your own well being to live happily ever after. Allowing yourself to be financially dependent on any one is foolish. Women comprise three-fifths of all people living in poverty in the USA. Due to divorce, death of a spouse, or spinsterhood, the majority of American women will at some point in their lives be solely financially responsible for themselves. Eighty percent of women die single. Eighty percent of men die married.

Powerless women frequently blame their gender or circumstances for their lack of power. You are responsible for your destiny. Neither gender nor circumstances can hold a woman back if she knows the steps required to find or create the circumstances that will lead her to the success she wants.

Three core steps are necessary to reach success in the jungle. First, you must clearly and succinctly define your goals. To do this you need to know two things. Ask yourself the following two questions and be honest with your answers. Where are you? Where do you want to go? Take a personal inventory of your current skills, experiences, background and education. Before you begin your journey, you must have 100% clarity of your desired outcome. Your objective is to define your journey from where you are now to where you want to be. Clarity in knowing where you currently are and clearly knowing where you want to go will drive you consciously and subconsciously to take the steps you need to reach your goals.

Mull over your answers. Define your journey. Commit your plan to paper. Don't go into the jungle without taking a moment to write down in 25 words or less where you want to go. Be clear. Be concise. Be exact. Simple clarity is incredibly powerful. This act of writing down where you want to go will send a message to the subconscious part of your mind to prime it to discover the path you should take to reach your destination.

To get what you want, need, and deserve you must take complete charge of your destiny. Once you establish a lifetime plan for where you want to go, you can determine the steps to reach your goal. Obstacles will arise that will throw you if you don't have a clear goal with a defined plan.

Listen to yourself. Tune in to those you trust. Tune out everyone else. Hear the song in your heart and listen to its rhythm. Listen to your song and do your own dance. Other people have their own tunes and their own dances. Dance to **your** song.

The purpose of this book is to equip you with the skills you need beyond your education and technical skills *"To go from Plain Jane to Getting What You Want, Need, and Deserve"* in the business jungle—and in life. If you care about the issues that affect your life as a woman wanting to survive in the business jungle, this book is for you. Grab your lipstick and let the safari begin!

Ready, Aim, ROAR!

An uninformed woman is like a stick of dynamite;
she has power inside
but nothing happens until her fuse is lit.

—*Jane Hight McMurry*

Chapter Two

Born to be Wild:
I am Woman, Hear Me Roar in a
Polite Yet Powerful Manner

I'm tough, ambitious and I know exactly what I want.

—*Madonna*

We are born wild. We come into this world not knowing how to walk, talk, or forage. We arrive uncivilized. We cry to get what we want. But there is no crying in the boardroom. Business people pounce on sensitive women. As women, we must roar to get our way. This book is about roaring in a powerfully polite and positive way to get what you want as a woman.

According to the U.S. Census Bureau, women still earn only $.78 to every man's dollar and fewer than 3% of Fortune 1000 CEOs are women. The reality remains that women are treated differently in the workplace in the way they are judged, rewarded, and punished despite advanced education, high-level skills and laws to ensure equal rights and opportunity. This book answers the question, "What else do women with competitive education and technical skills guaranteed equal rights under the law need to do to get what they want?"

Powerful women must roar differently from men if they are to reach the top of the mountain. Men are typically groomed to be competitive while women are not. In fact, women who assume a competitive demeanor are frequently branded as controlling and difficult. A man doing what he needs to in order to get what he wants is respectfully referred to as a "powerful man" while the same people often refer to a woman doing the same thing as the "powerful man" as a "bitch." Insecure people have a vested interest in squelching educated and skilled females who they perceive as competition in the workplace. Women need knowledge to walk the fine line that will propel them forward instead of holding them back. A Lipstick Lioness is powerful and polite and a **B**abe **I**n **T**otal **C**ontrol of **H**erself.

One of the first jungles I went into was far from my parent's friendly home. My goal at the time was to earn a degree in English and Dramatic Art. Part of this journey included an opportunity to study Shakespeare at Oxford University. Before I left for England, my mother took me shopping for the things I would need at Oxford. They included clothes, books, and a tube of pink lipstick. I vividly recall her taking me to The Intimate Bookshop in Chapel Hill, NC where we purchased not only the works of Shakespeare that I'd be studying at Oxford but also Cliff Notes to help me with my studies. You can imagine my surprise just before I boarded the plane when my mother wagged her finger at me and said, "You flunk that course. There is more to learn in England than what you can get from books." She was right!

At Oxford, people were from all over the world and they did not share the same customs I'd learned growing up in a small southern town. The Oxford Don and my fellow students looked at me curiously when they heard my southern accent in the drawing room where we learned and in the formal dining room when they observed the way I held my knife and fork. My mother had carefully drilled customs and courtesies into me since I was a child so I was surprised that perceptions about me were not favorable. This perception impeded my success. I telephoned home. My mother laughed and said, "Go buy one of their books on customs."

I walked down the street from St. Benet's College of Oxford University to Blackwell's Bookshop where I purchased a small yellow and black book about British customs. It was the first time I'd ever thought about learning different customs to help me accomplish my goals. I didn't flunk the Oxford course I'd come to study, but truly, I needed more than the tube of lipstick and the books I'd taken with me to survive and thrive in the jungle at Oxford!

Your favorite color of lipstick is a nice take-along into the business jungle, but to be a success in the corporate world you need more than one nice color of lipstick. Just as you have lots of items in your makeup case, you need lots of interpersonal skills to shine. Rather than mask yourself with color, you need skills that show off all of your assets. I am not talking about your booty! You need to know yourself and equip yourself with the skills you need to survive and thrive.

Your business life is a journey of self-discovery. To become a successful businesswoman, take a moment to assess your education, technical skills, and business communication savvy. Do you have the knowledge and skills required to enter the particular feeding ground you want to enter? Do you accurately translate who you are and your capabilities?

According to a *Fortune* magazine survey, 77% of successful women believe that women need to have more experience or higher degrees than men when applying for the same job as a man. Forty-three percent of the men surveyed agreed. When asked if women were satisfied with the overall status of women in the workplace, 61% of the men believe that women are satisfied, while only 44% of the women agreed.

If you don't have the skills you need—*get them.* Knowledge is power. As you go through life you may lose your parents, your boyfriend, your husband, your friends, your home, your car, your job. But if you have an education, no matter what happens, no one can ever take it away from you. Many jobs require formal degrees. No matter how much experience you have, many doors will remain locked to you if you do not have the formal education required. Make sure you have the key when you stand at the door of opportunity.

Keep learning after you've earned your formal degree. The skin of a dead sheep received at graduation will not keep your mind alive forever. Read everything you can get your hands on. Powerful women know that knowledge is power. Good luck occurs when preparation and opportunity meet. Be prepared for the opportunities that await you by equipping yourself with as much education and as many skills as you can so you'll be prepared to grab the horns of a charging ram.

Education is integral but it is not all that is required. It is up to you once you have knowledge to translate that you are competent and can do the job. It's 100% up to you to communicate your message, but the best you can ever do is your 50% of every opportunity you have to convey your message. What I mean by this is that communication is two-way. It requires a sender (you) and a receiver.

Communication begins before you arrive and it continues after you leave. Think about the book you are holding. What made you decide to read it? Probably you heard me speak, heard someone talk about the book or me, or read about the book or me. Most people go into a bookstore to buy a particular book—they seldom go into a bookstore to buy a book they haven't heard of by an author whose name they don't recognize. When they do buy a book they haven't heard of, it's likely because of its cover.

People often pick who they do business with the same way they pick the books they read. First, they receive advance information and if that is favorable, they invest time learning more about them in order to decide whether to buy their products or do business with them. A resume, a letter of recommendation, a phone call are all like a book review.

When a first time meeting occurs it is like looking at a book for the first time. The front cover is important. Buyers of books spend only three to five seconds looking at the front cover. The cover is what initially catches the eye. If buyers like what they see, they flip the book over and read the back cover for ten to fifteen seconds. If and only if they like what they see and read, they thumb through the pages, reviewing chapter titles, clarity, readability (including font size), and a glimpse of content. If upon cursory inspection the potential buyer determines the writer has something valuable to offer and can maintain the reader's interest, he will buy the book. Like it or not, that is how it is often done in business.

People make purchasing decisions within sixty seconds. It's scary, but that's what happens. What are you doing to improve your ability to convince others at the outset that you are the person who can best accomplish the job? And if you are initially successful, do you know how to ensure others that you can grow in the job you are entrusted to do? It's important to demonstrate that you have the technical and interpersonal skills to develop, maintain, and grow business.

Maybe some of you remember the Toni commercial from years ago. A young girl with my name, Jane, with straight hair and flat vocal expression flashes on the screen. Jane gets a Toni permanent which instantly transforms her into an ebullient young girl with a mop of gorgeous curly hair. She joyfully boasts, "I used to be a plain Jane, but now I'm beautiful!" The ad convinced my mother. My mother saw that commercial, went to the corner drug store, bought a Toni permanent and harnessed me to a high stool at my grandmother's house where she and my beloved Aunt Marstee rolled tiny pink rods in my hair and soaked my head with the most horrible smelling solution imaginable. The smell of the chemical was strong. I had to hold a towel over my face not only to diffuse the odor but also to keep the burning chemical solution they squeezed over the thin pink rods from dripping down my face and into my eyes.

That was a time when women often relied on looks to get what they wanted—usually a husband who could support them. Some women still have the notion that attracting a man with their looks is the best and easiest way to get what they want, need, and deserve. My readers—those interested in getting what they want, need, and deserve know that while good hair is a part of their "cover," hair is just one tool of many. Smart women use many tools and they fully understand that to get a job, keep a job, and advance in a job it takes more than beauty and stylish hair. *"A Man Is Not A Financial Plan,"* writes Candace Bahr, certified financial advisor and president of WIFE.org (Women's Institute for Financial Education) who teaches women how to manage their money. Take time to learn to manage money. Participate in managing money if and when you marry.

When another Jane, Jane Fields, CEO of MacDonald's was interviewed on NBC News with Brian Williams, she said that she started at the bottom of her company and worked her way up the corporate ladder. She was articulate and appeared every inch the cutting-edge corporate skirt that she was wearing in the interview. *Forbes* magazine includes her in its list of the fifty most powerful women in the world. It is no coincidence that during the NBC Nightly News interview she was wearing a cutting-edge corporate skirt—a black St. John knit to be exact. Look her up yourself. She looks like she can do the job—and she does it!

Being equipped with the right skills as well as packaging and promoting yourself are important to success. A *Washington Post* experiment about people's perception, taste, and priorities supports this premise. On January 12, 2007 in the DC Metro Station at L'Enfant Plaza, a violinist casually dressed and wearing a baseball cap played six pieces of Bach music for 43 minutes during which time over 1000 people passed through the station. After three minutes, a single middle-aged man slowed his pace and paused. After four minutes, a woman placed one dollar in the violinist's hat and continued on her way. After six minutes, a young man leaned against a wall and briefly listened before continuing to walk. After ten minutes, a three-year old boy stopped but his mother pulled him along. This happened with several other children whose parents wouldn't let them stop. After 43 minutes, only six people had stopped to briefly listen. Twenty people had given a total of $32.17. After an hour, the musician stopped playing. No one noticed. No one applauded. The musician received no recognition.

The violinist was Joshua Bell, one of the finest violin virtuosos of our era who was playing some of the most beautiful and intricate pieces of music ever written. His instrument was one of the finest ever made—a Stradivarius made in 1713 for which Bell had paid 3.5 million dollars. Only three nights before Joshua Bell had filled Boston's Symphony Hall where audience members had paid an average of $100 a ticket.

Consider the very different response to the free public concert if the event had been properly packaged and promoted. Packaging and advance promotion can make or break your career. You can be as talented in your field as Joshua Bell is in his, but if you don't take care to package and promote yourself for success, you will likely earn a pittance of what you are worth. It's essential that you equip yourself with the skills you need, package, promote, tell and remind people of what you want in order to get what you want.

Closer to home, I'm watching the way my own daughters are using the tools they need in the lipstick jungle to reach their goals. They continue to learn in school and on the job, work hard, and use acquired interpersonal skills.

I'll illustrate what you need to do to land the job of your dreams by telling the story of how my daughter, Win, got to wear the corporate skirt of her dreams as an anchor and reporter in the male dominated PGA Tour golf world.

Win attended the University of North Carolina at Chapel Hill where she worked on dual degrees in communication studies and journalism with a public relations track. Her senior year she took a sports writing class and loved it. Her professor told her that she had talent and should pursue a career in sports writing and broadcast journalism. The obstacle for Win was that it was too late to change her journalism track to broadcast journalism in time to graduate.

After graduation, Win moved to New York City. The same professor who encouraged her gave advice to her class during his final lecture of the semester. He said to make a plan, write it down, and to pack lightly when you move to start your job. Win moved to NYC with one suitcase, her laptop and a planner in which she'd written her goals and her plan. She had experience in PR but not in sports broadcasting and since the most important thing for her was to get a job and start working in the corporate world, her resume caught the initial attention of a Manhattan PR firm. She interviewed and got the job. She had the set of tools to get that job but it was not the job she wanted. She used the skills she had to position herself for another job. In addition to her education, she had a strong desire to succeed and a strong set of interpersonal skills. She needed to find a way into the sports broadcasting industry. What ended up opening the door for her came from a conversation she had with a fellow UNC alumnae she met at a networking event in New York City.

Win struck up a conversation with an older alumnae. They talked about what they were each doing. Win shared her goal—to work in sports broadcast journalism—with the alumnae. The woman told her that she had a friend who worked at CBS Sports who might be willing to speak to her. This college connection introduced her to her contact at CBS Sports. Win asked the new contact she made about his job at CBS Sports, how he got his start, what advice he could offer, and for help getting a job. She expressed her interest in work as an intern on the weekends in order to gain experience. As it happened, the new connection knew CBS Sports was looking for freelancers to work weekends in research scoring games. Win was offered a job.

Working both her full-time job and on the weekends for CBS Sports, she began looking for a way to make her work at CBS full-time. Housed in the studios with CBS Sports is the local station WCBS-TV. Win walked over and introduced herself to the Sports Director. She talked to him about her desire to work in sports broadcasting and gain more experience. They were looking for a script supervisor and field producer for the morning show which required a 3:30 a.m. call time. Win was eager to accept the job when it was offered even though it meant ending her PR job and taking a cut in pay. To supplement her reduced salary, she worked as a waitress in a restaurant and as a freelancer for another PR firm. Win worked seven days a week. It was a grueling schedule that required her to work long hours that had her sleeping on the floor of the edit room many nights at WCBS. Nevertheless, she grinded through it because she knew it was helping her reach her goal.

Win is a sports fan, especially a North Carolina Tar Heels sports fan. When the Carolina versus Duke basketball game rolled around she asked the production manager if she could go with the crew on-site to Chapel Hill as an unpaid assistant. He agreed and Win worked the game for free. Afterwards she was asked to help with the NCAA Tournament. When basketball season ended, she was asked to help with coverage of PGA Tour golf. Win recognized the opportunity and quit her other jobs in New York City to travel with CBS

Sports coverage of the PGA Tour. That job positioned her for a role at PGA Tour Entertainment as producer and on-air talent. She accomplished this by age 24. That is how it is done: education, interpersonal skills, creativity, and a willingness to work hard and to do whatever it takes while maintaining integrity.

Win rose to the top of her niche at the PGA Tour and at age 26 was offered a position as a broadcast journalist for Golf Channel. Her success is the result of mastery of many skills and an abundance of hard work.

Women often fail to get what they want, need, and deserve because they are afraid of stepping out of their comfort zone and taking risks. Growth, discovery, and adventure will be your rewards when you approach the business jungle by actively making the decision to get what you want, need, and deserve. Creating a written plan to reach your goals with small steps as part of your plan is important to getting what you want because "inch by inch life's a cinch. Yard by yard, life is hard."

Many women frequently remain in assisting positions when they are equally prepared as men awarded jobs they want because they continuously accept extra work and supportive roles rather than express interest in leadership roles. The feminine assets of compassion and attentiveness that make a woman a great secretary also make a great CEO. Speak up. Accept jobs that facilitate reaching your goals, not assisting jobs that brand you when you are ready for more. Speak up. Do not settle for less than you want when you are prepared, qualified, and desire more responsibility.

Say exactly what you want. The more precise you are, the more likely you are to get it. Many women are taught as little girls that it is impolite to ask for something and to wait until things are offered. That's hogwash when it comes to business. If you don't ask for what you want, you will likely never get it. My mom, Joan Williams Hight, drilled these words into me, "The meek might inherit the earth, but it's not going to be in your lifetime." Cowards never climb the corporate ladder.

Teach your daughters this. For example, if your daughter wants to ask Santa for a doll you have an opportunity to teach her this technique to increase her chance of getting exactly what she wants when she wants it. If she wants the Molly, Josefina, or Kanani doll from the American Girl Collection, coach her to ask Santa for the specific doll by name. For example, coach her to say, "I want The American Doll named Molly wearing the green velvet dress this year for Christmas under my Christmas tree." Explain to her that if she is not specific, she might get Barbie wearing a swimsuit for her birthday in July. Use the opportunity to teach her to always say not only what she wants but also how, when, where she wants it!

It's easier for people to give you what you want than to spend time guessing what you want. Help them. In *The Wizard of Oz,* The Gateman gives Dorothy what she wants when she finally provides him with the information to get what she wants. "Well, bust my buttons. Why didn't you say that in the first place? That's a horse of a different color! Come on in." Gain entrance by saying what you want.

Be clear. Be precise. Here is an example of what you might say when talking to a person who can offer you a job you want. *"I am interested in working in your office as a* _____ *and would like to discuss how I can help with* _____ *. Would it be possible to get together next week? Thank you for your time and interest."* That way the potential employer clearly knows four things you want:

1. A job

2. To learn his needs

3. To help with _____ and

4. A time that you'd like to get together.

Many employers continue to assume that a woman is not interested in opportunities for jobs that require a move to a new location or extra work hours because she may become pregnant or already has children. Do not be guilty of reflecting the definition of the word "assume" with your employer: *to make an "ass" out of "u" and "me"* by failing to let your employer know your goals and your willingness to do what is needed to meet the demands of a job with increased responsibilities. Let your employer unequivocally know what you want and that you are ready to accept additional responsibilities and are willing to relocate—whatever it takes in order to grow in your career.

You are 100% responsible for the message you send to other people so tell your employer that when new opportunities arise for which you are qualified that you'd welcome consideration. If you do not, your potential employer might put you off, forget about you, offer you a job you do not want, or offer the job you want to someone else. Remember the Gateman of Oz. It is your fault if you are an "ass" and fail to tell the Gateman that you're a "horse of a different color." You'll prevent the Gateman from being an "ass" if he erroneously assumes that because you're a woman you want to be reined back. You must politely give the uninformed Gateman the information he needs to open the door for you if you want to get what you want. Be smart. Be nice. Be clear. *Politely roar to get what you want!*

People will say, "We'll get back to you." When they do say that, respond enthusiastically, "Great! When do you think you'll be available?" It's pushy, but it's okay. Put the date they say on your calendar and if they don't call you, call them. Randy Pausch, the Carnegie Mellon professor and author of *The Last Lecture* said, "If you don't get a response within 48 hours, then it's okay to nag them." Be polite. When you follow up with people who haven't responded, say something like, "I haven't heard from you and just wanted to check back with you today as I remembered you saying you'd be ready to move forward this week. I am really interested in helping with the project and don't want to be off your radar." Being persistent will show that you're really interested and they will like that. Remember, "The meek might inherit the earth, but it's not going to be in your lifetime." Don't hesitate to let people who can help you reach your goals know what you want. Don't hesitate to ask people for what you want. The worst that can happen is that they will say no.

Always say *clearly what you want* and you'll increase your chance of getting exactly the doll you want, wearing exactly what you want it to wear, exactly when you want it. Passive management of your goals will get you nowhere. Be proactive. Ask for what you want, need, and what you deserve.

Be positive, remain positive, and persevere. Powerful women highlight their accomplishments, smile, and graciously say "thank you" when complimented. I repeat, say THANK YOU when you are complimented. DO NOT deflect or cheapen a compliment. Simply say THANK YOU. A compliment is a gift. Graciously accept it. Never ever say, "Oh it was nothing."

Powerful women do not tout their weaknesses or mistakes—nor do they downplay their successes. Let people who can help you know about your accomplishments in an artful and tasteful manner. Document your accomplishments and don't shy from saying you're good at something when it is helpful to others. Documentation is a powerful tool that lets others know your competence. Regularly update your resume so you won't forget what you've accomplished and as a reference for others to see your experience and accomplishments. This will help them...and it will help you. Visible displays of rewards, trophys, and certificates are reminders of your ability and accomplishments.

Surround yourself with positive people. Stay away from toxic people whose favorite party is a pity party with talk against almost everything and chatter full of "couldda shoudda woulddas and I'm so sorrys." Energy sucking vampires drain power.

Many women ritually self-deprecate by saying "I'm sorry." Accepting blame when you are not at fault relinquishes your power and weakens your professional image. In the words of Lois Wyse, American advertising executive, "Men are taught to apologize for their weaknesses, women for their strengths." Don't self-deprecate. The business world is not a fairytale land of happily ever after. Despite women's right to vote and legislation to ensure fairness in the workplace, it is a myth that justice, equality, and entrance into high-powered industries exist. My younger daughter, Allison, shared a recent conversation with her father who is a head and neck surgeon. The story she shared illustrates the attitude of many people in the 21st century that strips women of power. In the conversation, Allison mentioned her interest in attending graduate school. Her unsupportive father made the comment that women should not be accepted into graduate programs like medical school at the same rate as men. His reasoning was that when most women marry they quit work to raise a family. He said that most female doctors who do return to practice medicine after marrying and having children only want to work part-time.

Allison did research on the "motherhood penalty" and "fatherhood bonus" to which her father subscribes. She found, according to research by Catalyst Inc, 83% of new mothers return to work within six months after childbirth, 17% stop working after childbirth, 72% of senior female workers are married, and 64% have children. According to the Bureau of Labor Statistics, 40% female workers have children under the age of eighteen. Allison began study for her Ph.D. the following semester.

Do not cave to unsupported chauvinistic rationale or let some men *and some women* hold you back from reaching your goals by accepting power-stripping thinking. Life and people in it, even those in your own family, are not always the way they should be. The way you respond to life and the people in your life is what will make the difference in your success. Don't waste time trying to change people or a company with a discriminatory attitude that historically does not embrace the talents of women like you. Identify people and businesses that realize your value, are supportive, and will provide an opportunity for you to excel and be productive. Go there.

Do not doubt yourself. Do not give up. Persevere. The difference between a successful person and a failure is that the successful person got up the last time he or she was knocked down. The difference in having power and not having power is very small. To illustrate this point, think about the difference in very hot water and boiling water. At 211° water is hot. At 212° it boils. One tiny degree makes all the difference. A small extra degree of effort in your personal and professional life will make a difference in your ability to achieve your goals. The average margin of victory between winning and losing is a small degree—frequently less than a second in every Olympic competition. The margin of victory for the last twenty-five years in all major golf tournaments is less than three strokes. You are responsible for your results. Go the extra degree. As Walter

Elliot said, "Perseverance is not a long race, it is many short races one after another." Persevere one step at a time. Turn up the heat as little as one degree to get the power to get what you want.

We can lie in the language of dress or try to tell the truth;
but unless we are naked and bald,
it is impossible to be silent.

—*Alison Lurie*

Chapter Three

Smoke Signals:
Jungle Protocol

I speak two languages, Body and English.

—Mae West

According to Andrew Carnegie, "There are four ways, and only four ways, in which we have contact with the world. We are evaluated and classified by these four contacts: *what we do, how we look, what we say, and how we say it.*"

Let's start with *what we do.* Everything about you sends a message to the people who might want to hire you, promote you, or do business with you and your company. According to research conducted by Albert Mehrabian, we judge a person and form an opinion within the first sixty seconds of the initial meeting. A poor first impression can take a lifetime to undo. Be sure that everything about you is sending the signal you want. Research shows that 93% of our communication is nonverbal. Your signals include more than your words and the sound of your voice. Your signals include what people see.

Words account for only 7% of your message. Your posture, the way you sit and stand, the gestures you use, distractions you carry (cell phones, PDAs, newspapers, books or magazines), the non words (e.g. uhs, ands, etc.) you utter, give accurate or inaccurate clues as to your competence. Be careful what you carry! Understanding the signals and knowing how to respond to signals you receive will help you get what you want, need, and deserve.

In the 1870s, Morse Code was the most sophisticated mode of long distance communication. Morse Code positions were highly sought as they paid well and were prestigious. A company advertised for a new hire Morse Code operator. A young woman went to apply for the job. When she entered the office, she walked over to the reception desk where a sign read, "Thank you for coming to apply. Please sign in, take a seat, and wait to be called into the inner office for an interview."

The young woman signed the sheet of paper and took her seat in the waiting room filled with applicants. After about a minute and a half, the young woman rose from her seat and walked into the inner office.

The other applicants in the waiting room were angry that the young woman had jumped in front of them and began making comments like, "Who does she think she is?" "Can you believe the arrogance of that woman?" Another said, "Well, she'll never get the job. People like that are always found out."

In a few minutes, the president of the company emerged from the inner office with the young woman. The president said, "I appreciate your interest in the job. The job has been filled. Thank you for coming." An uproar began with people yelling and saying, "That's not fair!" "We were here first and waited for our turn." "She jumped ahead of us for an interview!"

The president put up his hands for them to calm down and said, "While you were waiting, a Morse Code message was being sent through the air. It said, 'If you can understand this message, come inside. The job is yours.'"

The applicants lost their chance for a well paying job because they failed to know the signals. Know the signals sent to you.

In addition to understanding signals sent to you, you need to be aware of the signals you send. People subconsciously consider your nonverbal signals to make judgments about your socio-economic and educational background. They make decisions about you based on the clarity and effectiveness of your actions, as well as your choice of words. You will appear more authoritative and confident the less you rely on gestures. In fact, studies show that the higher individuals are on the socioeconomic scale, the fewer gestures they use because they rely more on vocabulary to send messages. Extraneous gestures often compensate for a limited vocabulary. Increase your vocabulary through reading, listening carefully to others, and incorporating new words into your speech. Smearing your presence with non-words and distractions can overshadow your message. Ralph Waldo Emerson was right when he wrote, "What you *do* speaks so loud that I cannot hear what you say."

What are you *doing* when you enter the jungle? What can you be doing to win in the workplace? Sometimes we see and send signals without realizing their meanings. Here are a few of the most common examples.

Open Posture is the first thing people notice about your appearance. To show that you are confident, stand up straight. You can easily check your posture with a simple technique. Stand up. Stand straight with your legs six to eight inches apart. Position your chin so that it is parallel to the floor. Your posture should now be in alignment. Keep your chin parallel to the floor. Now lace your fingers behind your back. This pulls your shoulders back and down. Release your hands and place them by your side. Voila! Your posture is perfect. Do this until you get the feel of it and keep doing it throughout the day. Erect posture will do more for your presence than anything else will. Watch royalty walk. You will see royals frequently place their hands behind their backs to adjust their posture. It's not a coincidence that Prince Charles and Queen Elizabeth look like royalty. You too need to look like the queen!

Keep your body posture open and ready to move forward to show that you are ready to take on responsibility. Folding your arms in front of your body makes you look like you are protecting yourself or are cold. This body position physically appears to be blocking the conversational partner from you and therefore sends the subliminal message that you are not interested in conversation.

Placing hands on the hips indicates dominance and perhaps communicates that there are "issues."

Leaning against a wall, table, or chair translates a sloppy and casual attitude.

Shoving hands into a shirt, blouse, jacket or pocket makes the communicator appear more than non-professional. It may be interpreted that the communicator is secretive and may not want to openly communicate. After all, hands deeply thrust into the pockets are not available for shaking or for any other form of tactile communication. Preoccupation with money (either too much or not enough) is another interpretation when the hand in the pocket jingles loose change.

Stand Up! Cutting-edge corporate women know that *standing up* shows self-respect and respect for others. Gone are the days the fairer sex remained seated and waited until properly introduced to speak to others. STAND UP! Always stand up. Powerful women stand up.

How to Sit. Choose a rigid chair when you sit because it is difficult to look perky and powerful when you are swallowed by an oversized piece of furniture. Have a powerful sitting posture by approaching your chair and finding the chair with the back of your legs. Sit on the chair's edge and slide your hips back. Sit up straight. Place your feet properly with either both feet flat on the floor, crossed at the ankles, or crossed at the knees. Be aware that you run two risks when you cross your legs at the knees—varicose veins and appearing nervous if you swing your legs.

How to Place Your Feet. Showing the soles of your feet is an insult in some cultures. An embarrassing international incident occurred during a meeting between Russian President Nikita Khrushchev and Richard Nixon when Khrushchev crossed his legs and turned up his foot revealing a large hole in the sole of his shoe. The faux pas was reported all over the world by the international press and the editors of the *New York Times* chastised him for his bad manners. Be careful of the message you send—even with your feet. Look at signals sent by royalty in their portraits and remember to keep both feet parallel with your toes pointed in the same direction when you sit.

Tucking one foot underneath your body when sitting will make you appear ungrounded and girlish. Appear grounded by placing both feet on the ground.

Crossing the leg over the thigh is called the "know-it-all" position. It is a seated position more common with men than women, but because some women do sit like this, it needs to be mentioned. People who sit like this rarely change their minds especially if they place their hands behind their heads. Don't bother trying to bring a person sitting like this around to your way of thinking when you are in the dealing phase of business communication.

Crossed arms and/or legs tend to indicate a defensive frame of mind and placing a hand over the mouth or chin are signs of a person deep in thought. These body positions do not invite contact. Invite contact by keeping your arms loose by your side and keeping your hands away from your mouth.

Lean forward when you speak to others. This demonstrates interest and shows that you are listening.

Smile. Smiling requires the use of fewer facial muscles than frowning. A smile is the greatest indication of a friendly and positive attitude and a willingness to communicate. Your smile will make the other person feel more receptive towards you. No color of lipstick can do as much for your face as a smile.

AND ABOUT YOUR LIPSTICK! Apply it like insect repellent *BEFORE* you venture into the jungle. Go back into your tent to apply it. *DO NOT, REPEAT: DO NOT APPLY LIPSTICK while you're meeting and greeting* in the jungle or sitting by the campfire at a dinner table. Top-drawer corporate men don't groom at the table—savvy corporate women don't either. The same goes for powdering your nose, brushing your hair, and picking your teeth! Retreat to the privacy of your tent for all grooming.

Look people in their eyes. It is the custom in North America to look communication partners (CPs) in their eyes 40-60% of the time and to let the eyes travel around their faces the rest of the time. In our culture, we usually look directly in our CP's eyes for 5-7 seconds and then let our eyes travel around our CP's face, perhaps gazing at the forehead, cheek, and chin. Look at the other person's face at approximately five-second intervals to avoid seeming to stare them down which will make them uncomfortable and make you appear critical. Do not look the person up and down to check clothing as it will seem that you are judging the person.

Pay constant attention and do not look over the person's shoulder and around the room. Do not gaze away while your CP is speaking. When you talk, continue to look your CP in the eyes but also look away from time to time when you are thinking of your words. Never look away to check out who is in the room to determine who might be more interesting or more attractive than your CP! You might notice someone, but you will lose credibility the instant your expression reveals that you are not focused on your communication partner. Show that you understand your CP by nodding from time to time.

Psychologist Jane Templeton shared her observations in her article, *"How Salesmen Can Find Out What's Really on a Customer's Mind."* She wrote, "If a prospect's eyes are downcast and face turned away, you're being shut out. However, if the mouth is relaxed, without the mechanical smile, chin is forward, he is probably considering your presentation. If his eyes engage you for several seconds at a time with a slight, one-sided smile extending at least to nose level, he is weighing your proposal. Then if his head is shifted to the same level as yours, smile is relaxed and appears enthusiastic, the sale is virtually made."

However, in some cultures, it is poor manners to look a person in the eyes because it is considered too personal to look into another's "window to the soul." Do your homework and learn about a person from another culture before your meeting.

Constant touching of a wedding band (especially when the communicator is discussing a spouse) is observed as a sign that the marital relationship is experiencing difficulty.

Holding hands or objects such as a briefcase or magazine in front of the body indicates an anxious person desiring a communication barrier. Pulling objects from a briefcase or purse when entering a room gives the message that the person is not prepared or may be stalling for time.

Spreading out when sitting sends off unfavorable messages for both men and women. However, the unfavorable message is different for each sex. The man who sits spreading out is signaling that he is taking over, while men interpret a woman who is spreading out as overstepping her bounds. However, if the woman places only one arm on a nearby chair the nonverbal message is that she wants to be perceived as having equal authority. Women who want to be taken seriously generally find it useful to lean forward slightly while resting their elbows on the table and lightly clasping their hands. In addition, women who sit next to the most powerful person in the room are perceived to have power.

Quick paced walk accompanied by freely swinging arms suggests a person who is goal-oriented.

Walking with hands in the pockets as a habit suggests that the person is secretive and negative.

Walking with hands on the hips suggests a person who wants to cover the most territory.

Touch appropriately. In a business environment, touching others is generally inappropriate and can be considered offensive. Do not reach out and touch people you have just met, with whom you are not completely comfortable, or who are senior to you in your business. The only acceptable form of professional touch in North American business culture is the professional handshake.

In the United States, a handshake is used between people making a deal. The pledging of words between people who trust each other is valued more than many written contracts between people who distrust each other.

The handshake is the accepted greeting for men and women in almost every country around the world. Even the Japanese will bow and shake hands when beginning and ending a meeting in the Western world. Don't hold back—extend your hand immediately. You are judged by your handshake. Women take their place equally beside men. The woman's handshake, like a man's, should convey warmth and sincerity while making a positive, tactile connection with another person. Stand when you shake—it shows respect for others and respect for yourself. Powerful women stand when they greet people hello and they stand when they say goodbye. If a person is a visitor in your office or home, stand and walk them all the way to the door.

The weak limp fish handshake sends the subliminal message that the person is weak and looks to others to make decisions. The person who offers a weak shake is viewed as not truly interested in shaking hands and socially interacting.

The fingertip-extender handshake sends a subliminal message similar to that of the weak limp fish. Rendered more frequently by women than men, it almost appears to be extended for the purpose of receiving a kiss.

The bone-crusher handshake. This handshake's subliminal message is that the person is aggressive and seeking to intimidate. Further, the person may be viewed as angry. Sometimes the person giving this handshake will turn the hand so that it is on top of the other person's hand. This power play is read, "I'm on top." Remove rings from your right hand before entering into multiple handshaking situations to reduce risk of overly firm bone-crusher handshakes.

The gloved handshake (sometimes referred to as the preacher handshake) is given by placing the left hand on top of the shaking hands. It is effective for consoling but not for doing business.

The professional handshake is firm and web-to-web with three to four pumps from the elbow. Accompany your shake with a smile, direct eye contact, and open body posture.

Keep your right hand free–ready to give and to receive handshakes. A good professional handshake is dry and pleasant to the touch. Keep your shaking hand (the right hand) dry by not holding iced drinks with that hand and perhaps momentarily sticking your hand in your jacket pocket to warm it before shaking hands.

Some people are not comfortable shaking hands because they have hyperhidrosis, commonly known as sweaty palms. A secret tip is to keep a small powder puff or handkerchief in your pocket or purse so you can periodically touch it to absorb excess moisture. If your problem is severe, tell your physician who can prescribe a product called "drysol" which is very effective in eliminating the problem of sweaty hands. A new and simple surgical procedure performed by thoracic surgeons can eliminate hyperhidrosis.

If for some reason you cannot shake hands, explain it to the person who has extended his hand to you. For example, "I would like to shake your hand, but I sprained my wrist when I moved furniture, repaired the computer, fell off a horse at a dude ranch, ...etc." Comments such as these not only break the ice but also serve as excellent conversation bait.

Body language with physically challenged individuals is insightful. Remember that a person with a disability does not have a contagious disease and should never be pre-judged or defined by his disability.

Heavy fragrances should be avoided so you won't come on too strong when meeting people.

The hands can be effective in communicating ideas. It is important to be careful when using body language transculturally.

Pointing the finger at any one in any culture is likely to generate ill will. However, the fingers can be used effectively to reinforce communication that contains numerous items.

Using the fingers facilitates conversation that includes several points. Try to keep oral lists to three items as more than three increases the difficulty of oral comprehension. North Americans begin the count with the index finger, followed by the middle finger, and then the ring finger. Europeans typically begin enumerations with the thumb followed by the index finger and then the middle finger.

Removing clean eyeglasses to clean is viewed as a procrastination technique.

Placing eyeglasses in the mouth is thought to indicate that the person is either hungry or searching for additional information and is taking time making a decision.

Ear pulling, eye rubbing, nose rubbing, chin rubbing, and covering the mouth are interpreted by people who read body language to indicate concealment of information, uncertainty, or an untruth being spoken by the communicator. An analysis by neurologists and psychiatrists of President Bill Clinton's body language during his testimony to the Grand Jury regarding his extramarital affair revealed that Clinton did not touch his nose when he told the truth. However, when he lied, the analysis found that Clinton gave a split-second frown and touched his nose once every four minutes for a grand total of twenty-six nose touches.

Read body language in gesture clusters and consider the setting and the individual. For example, the person *rubbing his eyes and nose* may be demonstrating an allergic reaction to the cat in the room, not that he is hiding information from someone and cannot look at them. The person covering the mouth may be tired and not unintentionally conveying, "I shouldn't say that." The social yawn on the other hand can indicate more than fatigue. Often this person is trying to buy extra time when facing a mildly stressful situation.

Touching the hair or tossing it back implies that a person thinks positively about his or her personal appearance.

Twirling strands of hair indicates confusion, uncertainty and nervousness.

Running a hand through the hair generally conveys a sense of being unsure of what to say or do next. The professional woman who wears her hair up is conveying that she is in control or at least wants to be in control. Women who wear their hair down are generally perceived in a more sexual than professional way.

Stroking the chin is a promising sign that means the listener is interested.

Showing the hands palms up indicates an open and receptive communicator.

Steepling is the gesture of pressing the fingers together and resting the chin or mouth on the fingertips. This gesture indicates deep thought as though the communicator is praying for an answer. Additional interpretations, especially when read as part of a cluster of gestures involving posture and eye contact, suggests that the person is confident, proud, and perhaps pontifical. It is thought that the higher the position of steepling the more confident the person is.

Tugging at the collar is an indicator that the communicator's body temperature has increased. Yes, it might be hot in the room, which does need to be considered, but the person who knows how to read nonverbal communication is also aware that body temperature increases when people lie. A hand automatically reaching up to let air in by loosening the collar may mean that a person is hot under the collar because he is nervous or anxious.

Stroking a scarf (or stroking a necktie for men) is a nonverbal signal that the communicator is trying hard to please and is desirous of making a good impression.

Jiggling the foot back and forth when the legs are crossed, tapping the foot on the floor exudes nervousness.

Biting nails, twisting hair, cracking knuckles, and chewing gum show lack of poise and sophistication and thereby can subtly sabotage your career.

Giggling excessively and without reason is conversational filler that denotes nervousness and anxiety. It is often a weak ploy to gain acceptance. Powerful women do not inappropriately giggle.

Reading the body language of others is an inexact science made even more difficult when we consider that nonverbal signals vary from city to city, state to state, and country to country. However, because people do read each other, it will serve you well to be aware of some of the most common nonverbal signals you may receive in the business world. In addition, knowing how body language is perceived will help you to send signals that will equip you with the tools you need to get what you want, need, and deserve.

A handsome young man born and raised in Spain shared his story with me one day after a training class I conducted for a global consulting company based in the United States.

I moved to this country to attend the University of Virginia where I played golf on the UVA team. When I lived in Spain, I did well

*in school. My teachers liked me. I had many
friends. I never had difficulty getting a date.*

*I struggled to fit in for a long time at UVA,
never understanding that the way I success-
fully conducted myself in Spain was causing
me relationship problems in the United States.
In the United States, no one seemed to want to
be near me or have anything to do with me. I
became depressed. One day during golf practice, my golf coach came over to me and said,
'You are standing too close to people.'*

*What you are teaching is vital not only to
professional success in this country but also
to personal success.*

The young man was referring to the *interpersonal
zone or spatial distance* between communicators. The
average North American is most comfortable interacting with communication partners at a distance of 18
to 24 inches. The interpersonal zone varies within this
distance according to each individual's personality, self-
concept, and attitudes towards conversational partner,
cultural background, and perceived or real rank. In
addition, the study of proxemics shows that extroverts
and people with high self-esteem tend to stand closer to
a conversational partner within the acceptable range
while introverts and people with low self-esteem stand
on the outer limits of the acceptable peripheral range.
Note that a regional spatial zone that is closer or greater
than your culture's acceptable zone can cause miscom-
munication. For example, conversational partners in

the Middle East, Southern Europe, and Latin America typically converse while standing closer together than people from Northern Europe and North America.

The business world is global. Take time to learn about your communication partner's customs which are often different from your own. Know the culture of your conversational partner in advance when possible. Skilled safari guides will quickly tell you to be quiet and to look for silent signals in the jungle. Learn the signals. Read the signals of the people in your business jungle. Be aware of the signals you send.

Slightly tilting the head can indicate that the listener is interested in what he hears. Charles Darwin first noted this in animals as well as humans. Frequently *tilting the head* to the side when listening is most often interpreted as indicating submission. It is power depleting. Leave the head tilt to flirts.

Nodding the head periodically is an active listening technique in North America that shows approval, understanding, and that you wish the person to continue speaking. Nodding too frequently is like wearing too much rouge—you'll look overdone and insincere as if you are not actually listening. The way a nod is given does not mean the same thing in every culture.

My daughter, Allison, recently traveled to India. When she arrived in Mumbai, she went to the airport's ATM machine to get money. A big burly guard holding an Uzi submachine gun stood in front of the money machine. She asked the guard if she could get money from the ATM. He bobbled his head right to left and said, "yes." The guard said yes, but his head to her understanding indicated no.

Allison respected his gun and did not want to misinterpret so she repeated her question. Again, the guard bobbled his head right to left while saying yes. Allison was perplexed and afraid to go past him. But she needed money. Therefore one final time she asked, "Are you sure it is okay for me to get money?" This time the guard barked, "Yes!" Allison got her money. It was a quick awakening for her that body language is different in different places in the world.

People like to do business with those they perceive to be like themselves, or at the very least, indicate an understanding of them. Take the time to learn about the customs of your CPs when you do business with global partners and show them that you understand their customs. The message you send when you do not know the communication customs is that perhaps you are stupid, ignorant, or simply don't care enough to learn the most basic things about them or their business culture. Equipping yourself with the tools you need in the business jungle can mean the difference in getting a job in the USA or being barked away in India!

While clothes may not make the woman,
they certainly have a strong effect on her self-confidence—
which, I believe, does make the woman.

—Mary Kay Ashe

Chapter Four

Safari Gear:
You Need More Than One Shade
of Lipstick!

*I have wondered how long men would retain their rank
if divested of their clothing.*

—Ralph Waldo Emerson

I went to the local post office to mail a letter. It was after hours and I was the only person in the lobby. One of the postal workers walked into the lobby and said, "Oh it's the competition." I looked up because I thought I was the only one in the post office. I turned to look behind me and saw no one. In a friendly voice the man said, "You're the competition." I looked puzzled. Suddenly I realized that I was wearing a brown blouse with matching brown trousers. He thought I was a UPS employee.

Business people consciously and unconsciously identify others by their clothing and make judgments accordingly—even before they speak. Leadership studies prove that people follow those who are well dressed in the style to which they aspire. Dressing in a manner that closely matches your communication partner is a powerful subliminal rapport building technique.

The clothing you select will send a message about you, so be careful to choose clothing that sends the message you intend. Do research before you dress yourself in the clothes already in your closet and before you make new purchases. Clothes are an important part of nonverbal communication and play a big part in establishing who you are, where you are from, and what you can do. Mark Twain said, "Clothes make the man. Naked people have little or no influence in society." Neither do people who wear the wrong clothes. You need to wear the right clothes. When building your wardrobe, buy quality over quantity. Shop early in the season so you can have more options. Classic colors such as black, gray, navy, beige, and taupe tend to have a longer wearing time than bright trendy colors. Find a good tailor and have your clothes properly altered. Trousers start at the natural waistline and break at the in-step. A good investment is a quality clothes brush. Dry clean and wash your clothes as little as possible to prevent them from looking limp—clothes quickly lose their sizing after cleaning.

Business clothing is not about personal style or comfort. Business clothing is about showing respect for others and the positions they hold. Jungle clothes are tools. If you're smart you'll put a lot of thought into the clothes you wear because it can be a factor to your success in business. Choose the business dress that is appropriate for your industry and the industry functions you attend. The business dress for your industry may require that you dress up or down in order to fit in with the people with whom you wish to do business.

If you are in doubt as to what to wear, it is appropriate to ask as it shows your interest in fitting in and being a team player.

Businesswomen are often confused about what to wear because dress codes vary in different business cultures in the United States and abroad. To further complicate what to wear, every business has a unique set of behaviors, protocols, and styles that define its culture. In the United States, we recognize three broad types of corporate culture, each with its own dress code. The three types are *conservative, modern,* and *unstructured.*

The first type of corporate jungle is the *conservative.* This jungle is characterized by an autocratic style of leadership. The environment exudes conservatism and its established patterns are slow to change. The atmosphere is quiet. Offices tend to be well designed and traditional. The mood is serious. Examples are old established law firms, banks, and blue chip companies that are very structured.

Conservative employees are businesslike. Conservative dress code tends to be formal. Women will likely be wearing suits in navy, black, or beige. Jackets are paired with skirts more than dresses or trousers. Skirt length is generally slightly below the knee or at the knee but rarely above the knee. Other colors may be worn, especially red as red and black are considered the ultimate power colors. The higher the quality of the fabric, the greater the range the suit color can be. If you are in this jungle, choose simple, well-cut suits or dresses instead of faddish items. Make sure undergarments are not showing and that clothes do not cling to your figure. Women's brightest clothing color in conservative business culture is typically splashed on with a scarf or blouse that does not reveal cleavage. Blouses are cotton or silk, most often white or pastel. Shoes are usually closed-toed with 1" to 2" low heels. Hosiery should be flawless (no runs) and conservative in color and in harmony with the shoes (no light hosiery with dark shoes.) Makeup is minimal—some mascara, no color shadow, soft rouge, powder, and lipstick. Hair tends to be short, but if it is long, it is pulled back and away from the face. Light brief case or portfolio case made of leather often is carried in place of or in addition to an unostentatious handbag that is usually small and in a dark color that matches the shoes. Jewelry is high quality, not flashy. You'll often see women wearing pearls, gold necklaces, earrings that do not dangle, and bracelets that do not make noise. There should be no visible body piercing (nose rings, eyebrow rings, etc.) Perfume should be so faint you need to be in an intimate interpersonal space to smell it.

The second type of corporate jungle is the *modern business culture*. Modern jungles are characterized by a team approach to management. The environment appears open to new ideas and exudes confidence. The furniture tends to be sleek and modern. Displayed artwork is colorful. Office doors generally are open. Examples are consulting, architectural and advertising companies. The employees appear friendly, approachable and helpful and often socialize after hours.

Professional dress in modern culture includes suits with color and relaxed styling or casual trousers, sport jackets, and day dresses. Shoes may be heeled, wedged or peep-toed, but not sandals. Shoe colors are generally limited to dark or neutrals. Legs may be bare especially if the shoe has a peep-toe. Hosiery is in tone with the shoes. Opaque hosiery has little or no design. Briefcases may be microfiber or leather. Handbags are stylish but for the most part unadorned. Makeup is polished and may have a slight shimmer that is missing in a conservative culture. Perfume is faint and minimal. Hair is groomed, close to the scalp, and in place whether short or long. Jewelry tends to be sleek.

The third and most chaotic of the jungles is the unstructured. *Unstructured business culture* is characterized by democratic leadership and because it is less structured it is difficult to read. One person may wear different hats. This may be a new organization which has not defined its structure or management approach. The rules are less defined and the noise level may be loud with audible music. There may be no set work hours. Office décor is not a priority and furniture may be mismatched due to changing styles and growth and may very well come from an attic. Examples are startup companies based in a garage or a business conducted from a spare bedroom.

Female employees in unstructured business cultures may appear casual and familiar. They do not wear suits or jackets but prefer slacks, jeans, or fun dresses. Shoes run the gamut from sandals, stilettos, to boots in all colors. Legs are often bare. Hosiery may be colored and textured. Briefcases are seldom carried but totes, hobo bags, textured leather, and cloth bags with decorations can appear. Makeup may be totally lacking or heavily applied. Body piercings may be multiple. Perfume or cologne may be obvious. Accessories are trendy, large, and often dangle.

The most important thing to remember when choosing clothing for your particular jungle is that in business, clothes serve the same purpose as a book's cover. Clothes are tools for sending messages. Use psychology. Let your clothes reflect who you are and the business you are capable of conducting. When you are in doubt, ask, and err on the side of formality when there is no one to ask. When purchasing business clothing, choose quality over quantity. The very best advice for dressing in your particular jungle is this: *Dress not for the job you have, but for the job you want!* You absolutely need to look the part. It's true, "Only birds with the right feathers are admitted to the nest."

     * Note: *Business casual is different for conservative, modern, and unstructured business cultures. However, every business casual look should include:*

- Good grooming, including clean hair and fingernails
- Clothing in good repair
- Well-maintained shoes appropriate for the job
- Appropriate hosiery or socks

The pendulum swings with clothing trends, as in all things, to both extremes and then back to the middle. Many companies are re-thinking, revamping, or completely abandoning dress-down policies initiated in the

1990s after discovering the downside of dress-down. A survey conducted by the employment law firm Jackson Lewis showed that 44% percent of the 1000 companies surveyed noticed an increase in tardiness, absenteeism and "flirtatious behavior" after implementing dress-down policies. An Incomm Center for Research and Sales Training poll revealed that less than half of trade show customers responded favorably to sales persons in casual attire, whereas 86% responded favorably to those dressed in business attire. Those statistics underscore the economic sense of the current return in many businesses to request formal business attire among those who interact with clients on a daily basis.

Try as we might, we cannot change the perception of others. Perception is reality. Dress-down attire sends the subliminal message that the person is thinking about herself, her comfort, and her convenience. Professional attire signals a woman in control with focus on business, the customer, and service to the customer. You need to look professional if you want to be perceived as a professional. Even in places where the rules have changed, the one thing that remains is the need to look professional, confident and competent.

Look professional at all times and remember that men are hard-wired. Your stylish professional outfit with a low neckline or tight hip fit may not look sexy to you or to other women. However, two legged males in the corporate jungle will see you the same way four legged males in the natural jungle see females. Males are visual. Don't lose power by losing sight of the perception created by your choice of clothing.

Shaunti Feldhahn, author of *"The Male Factor: The Unwritten Rules, Misperceptions, and Secret Beliefs of Men in the Workplace,"* conducted a study to test the difference in men's and women's perception of dress. He asked white-collared men and women what they think when they see a woman dressed in a way that emphasizes her figure. Seventy-six percent of the men surveyed believe a woman wants the men around her to look at her body while only twenty-three percent of the women surveyed agreed.

Consider the venue, the situation, the age and sophistication of the business people with whom you interact as you choose the proper clothing to help you send the message you intend. When you do choose to wear business casual clothing, remember it is always "business" first and "casual" second. Err on the side of formality. Casual Friday is not power friendly. It magnifies the differences in the way men and women are perceived. Men have the advantage of being able to wear khakis and a short-sleeved shirt and still look somewhat powerful. Casual wear options for women often send a powerless message. Women run the risk of sending the message that they are more interested and better suited for a party than for a leadership role when they wear heels that are too high, makeup that's a bit heavy or bright, etc.

What to wear into the jungle depends on the nature of the jungle. Not all businesses and not all jungles are the same. The jungle in Africa is different from the jungles in India and South America. The courtroom is different from the boardroom. Know your jungle before you head in to it. If you want to fit into a corporate setting, blend with the environment, but know when to be flexible. Carl Sandburg told a story about a chameleon who got along very well, adjusting moment by moment to his environment, until one day he had to cross a scotch plaid. He died at the crossroads heroically trying to blend with all the colors at once. Maintain integrity to the jungle you're in but be flexible enough to change when change is needed!

You need different tools and skills for different jungles. Consider the five high-power Ps: Prior Planning Prevents Poor Performance. To be successful in the jungle you must not only know yourself but also know the animals, their habitat, and their behavior.

Prepare every detail for high-power professional relationships. Before you go anywhere, consider who, what, when, where, why and how.

- Who are the participants?
- What is the purpose?
- When will you be there?
- Where will you be?
- Why are you going?
- How can you be the most effective in accomplishing your goals?

Detective work will pay off if you are unsure about the typical business attire for a particular industry. Ask around.

A large international consulting company I worked for headquartered in Washington, DC required consultants going into a new business to drive their cars to the place of business, sit outside, and observe the clothing people were wearing as they entered and exited the building and then dress accordingly to begin a business relationship. They knew that people like to do business with people they perceive as like themselves and that similar clothing is a subliminal way to minimize differences. Clothing is an easy way to establish that you fit in a particular jungle.

Finally, if you are going to an event and are unsure of the attire, call the host and ask. Don't be shy. Your call demonstrates initiative that shows you belong in the specific jungle.

Chapter Five

Wilderness Expeditions: Smart Travel in the Jungle

The world is a book and those who do not travel read only one page.

—*St. Augustine*

B e vigilant in the jungle. You never know who is hiding behind a bush. Avoid ambush by unexpected visitors and people who know you but whom you do not recognize. They pop out of nowhere— visiting in the next cubicle, sitting on the subway seat across from you, and reclining in the seat behind you on an airplane. To accomplish what you want, need, and deserve you need to be in total control of yourself and control the perception others have of you at all times. Your message—that you are capable of being queen of the jungle—must be consistent day in and day out.

Carefully choose your reading material when you're in public. Keep your conversation light. Politely disengage from conversation that is negative or unprofessional. Never discuss confidential business on public transportation.

Do not arrive or leave with anyone in a public place who could compromise your reputation. Things are not always as they seem, but in business and in life, perception is quite often the same as reality. Therefore, be aware of the perception others have of you from the moment you arrive until you make your exit.

According to a survey commissioned by *Fodor's* travel publications, 68% of people surveyed say they dress up for business and leisure travel because they receive better service from airline employees and hotel staff. Wear business casual clothing when you travel for business. Avoid sweat suits, jeans, shorts and tee shirts and be a bit reserved.

Show respect to senior members from your jungle when traveling by offering the preferred seat in a plane, cab, or car. The preferred seat in an automobile is the seat closest to the curb so the passenger does not have to slide over for others. In a plane, it is the aisle or window seat and the seat closest to the front of the plane. Ask the senior member if you are unsure which seat the senior member prefers. Respect and courtesy are recognized and appreciated.

Chapter Six

Where the Wild Things Are: Kings and Queens of the Jungle

Count to three. Get up, dress up, and show up because you never know who you might meet.

—*Martha Jane Roberts Williams*

Royalty is everywhere in the jungle. Look for it like a powerful predator. Your network in the jungle will give you power. Powerful people understand that power is in numbers. It's important to know where to look and how to cultivate a strong network that can support you and help you reach your goals.

In the past, men had exclusive clubs to help them control business and politics as well as to meet and develop relationships that would help them reach their goals. Rotary, Jaycees, Kiwanis, and Lions Clubs were the sole domains of men. I recall accompanying my former husband to a Rotary meeting where I was welcomed as a "Rotary Ann." Clubs are changing. Women are now welcomed as valued members in many clubs despite the tradition of being denied membership to others. Seek membership in forward thinking clubs.

Identify and join clubs in your community with missions you want to support. Your involvement will require an investment of your time, but you will be a better person for it. Attend meetings with the attitude that you will give before you get. Consider how you can be of assistance to the people you meet. You will reap the rewards of fellowship, friendship, and contacts that will enhance your personal and professional life.

Consider mixed gender groups and women's groups like the broad-based American Business Women's Association (ABWA), Association of Junior Leagues International (AJLI), Business and Professional Women (BPW), Executive Women International (EWI), National Association of Female Executives (NAFE), National Association of Women Business Owners (NAWBO), and niche groups like Women in Agriculture and the Women Lawyers' Association. All are terrific groups to join and begin your network.

Networking lionesses prowl the entire jungle. Don't overlook your church, your alumni association, and opportunities to meet people at museum or art openings. Don't limit yourself to who you talk to at these events by gravitating to women only or to people you already know. Connect with everyone—young, old, men and women as all kings and queens are royal connections in the networking jungle.

Power is in numbers, but only if you take the time to develop the connection into a relationship. Powerful networking takes time and is worth the investment. Your networking goal at meetings and events should not be to talk to as many people as possible, but to leave with one to five personal connections where you've taken the time to learn more about these individuals. You never know when you will meet someone who can help you reach your goals. Don't settle for interacting with the people who are the easiest to access. You need to reach outside your comfort zone because there you will find a wealth of new connections that will add power to your success.

Always be on the look out for new groups in new places in new jungles because if you always pick the same fruit from the same tree you'll eventually run out of fruit! Be active in your jungle, go places in different jungles, and try new activities wherever you go. You never know whom you will meet at a yoga class or a museum opening. Invest your time in everyone including people you think you will never see again because you never know the doors a new person can open.

We'd all like to think that we get what we want, need, and deserve because of our talent and abilities. However, we do not live in an ideal or fair world. It is often not what we know but who we know that is important. Further, it's an interesting fact that much of a person's success is frequently not due to a primary connection but to one that is once or many times removed. In other words, someone we know knows someone who knows someone who can help us. To have power you need connections. Build a strong network to become a powerful networking lioness.

According to Richard Wiseman, Ph.D., a professor at the University of Hertfordshire in England, the greater your network, the more opportunities you have. His research shows that the average person knows approximately 300 people by first name. He concludes that if you go to an event and meet someone new you will be "only two handshakes away from 300 times 300 people. That's 90,000 new possibilities for a new opportunity just by saying hello." If the yoga class or museum opening you attend attracts 50 people, you're just a couple of introductions away from millions of people who may be able to help you get what you want, need, and deserve.

Your network will wither and die if you do not feed it. People are just like animals that need to be petted and fed. Follow up with the people you meet by letting those you meet know that you care about them and appreciate them. Write personal notes, invite people in your network for coffee, a round of golf, etc. Danish comedian Victor Borge was on target when he said, "Visit people once a year."

Chapter Seven

Entering the Jungle:
Look before you Leap!

*Your manners are always under inspection by committees
little expected either awarding or denying great prizes.*

—*Ralph Waldo Emerson*

Your first responsibility when you are invited to any event is to respond. Respond to every event to which you are invited. If you're invited by telephone you can respond by telephone. If you are invited via formal invitation, respond with a formal reply. Failure to respond to an invitation shows lack of respect. Don't strip yourself of power before you arrive.

Social interaction is often the reason for business events. Many participants experience anxiety at the thought of facing a room full of people whether or not they know the people attending. Business and social events are places to connect with many people—not a place to have deep, meaningful conversations with just a few. Most conversations run their course in seven to eight minutes so while you might shake hands with more people, you'll likely have time for only seven to eight conversations per hour.

You need to master the fundamental skills so you can maximize your effectiveness for business opportunities. Entering a room correctly, making good introductions, and engaging in good conversation will help you attract, develop, and maintain business.

Wear a nametag when tags are available. Wear yours on the upper right shoulder so those you meet can easily read it. People shake hands right hand to right hand so the natural direction of the eyes is to the right shoulder. If possible, add one or two words about yourself below your name. (company, town, etc.) This information nugget will help others know you and can be a springboard for conversation.

Enter your jungle with purpose and be in charge of yourself. Most people walk into the work place, a business, or social event without prior planning for successful interaction. Walk through the doorway and then step to the side out of the traffic path. Pause and look around the room. Look for the big game—the key people you must speak to such as the host, an honored visitor, or a high-ranking official.

Look approachable, maintain good posture, and wear a pleasant facial expression. Few people will notice you do this, but if they do, so much the better, for this is the proper way to enter a room. Lower your volume when entering the room with others with whom you may already be engaged in conversation. Noisy conversationalists send the subliminal message that they have low self-esteem or are seeking attention.

If there is a receiving line, go through it early. If you arrive on time you will not have to waste time standing in a long receiving line to greet your host and any guests of honor who should be greeted when you first arrive. A receiving line is a courtesy established to make saying hello easy to those you must greet. You must go through the line.

Do not eat or drink until you've greeted the hosts even if you don't know them. A woman traditionally precedes her male escort through a receiving line. It is correct for the woman to introduce herself. If you bring a guest to the event, precede your guest and introduce your guest to the hostess who in turn introduces you to the guest of honor. Men precede women through receiving lines only if the event takes place at The White House, an all male campus, or a military event when the man is enlisted and the woman is not.

You will need to find the guest of honor, your boss, and your host when there is no receiving line. Wait for a break in conversation when you approach a guest of honor surrounded by many people and say something like, "Excuse me, I would like to introduce myself and to say hello..." Be careful not to monopolize the guest of honor or the boss who is generally in high demand. Shake the hand of the host and any honored guests (firmly, web to web) and tell them that you are delighted to be at the event. You do not need to engage in lengthy conversation because other guests will be waiting to say hello. Arriving on time is also beneficial because you can make maximum use of building and maintaining your network at the event.

Identify the people you want to speak to if you have time. You will want to determine if you have met the people on the list before and recollect what you know about them as you plan conversation with them at the party. Ask other people to share what they know about the guests you do not know who will be arriving. It is perfectly acceptable to telephone your host or the meeting planner of an event to ask who will be attending. This shows your interest in the other guests. It will help you with your conversation. Many business people I know prepare to meet others they will meet by doing a google search of the names of people they plan to meet.

The reason for your business event is meeting and greeting, so forage last at the oasis—or eat before you go! You will look like a cow chewing cud if you stand around grazing. If you want to eat, get a plate and start at the beginning of the buffet table. Do not overload your plate. Find a table after you've served your plate. Sit down to eat. If you want seconds from the buffet, get a clean plate and start back at the beginning of the buffet line without cutting in front of others for the specific food you want to replenish. If no waiter is available to clear your plate, look for a service table to put your dirty plate. A service table is a side table that is completely empty and is usually off to the sides of the room.

When you arrive at a table, speak to everyone seated at the table. Walk around the table to introduce yourself to people you do not know. This will distinguish you as someone who knows what to do. You'll be recognized as a leader when you do this. Be sure to give your first and last names and offer a small amount of conversation bait to the guests at your table. Shake hands firmly web to web while looking the person in the eyes.

Rise to greet others who arrive at your table after you are seated.

A host who carefully plans seating arrangements may indicate seats for guests to sit in by using place cards. Do not switch the cards. Sit in the seat a place card indicates for you to sit.

Good guests are not boorish. They participate in event activities. Learn to dance if you don't already know how to dance. Nobody cares if you can't dance well. Get up, dance, and have fun. Laugh at yourself and others will laugh with you and love you for not taking yourself too seriously. Finally, at the conclusion of the event, you must find your host to say "thank you" *plus one*. *Plus one* is adding to your thanks mention of at least one thing you especially enjoyed about the event. For example, "Thank you so much for including me. The fabulous band made dancing so much fun!"

Your own words are the bricks and mortar
of the dreams you want to realize.
Your words are the greatest power you have.
The words you choose and their use
establish the life you experience.

—*Sonia Croquette*

Chapter Eight

Talk to the Animals:
What to Say and How to Say It

If I could talk to the animals, just imagine it,
Chattin' with a chimp in chimpanzee,
Imagine talking to a tiger, chatting with a cheetah,
What a neat achievement it would be!

—Dr. Doolittle

The most important part of meeting and greeting is called the introduction. Social introductions differ from business introductions. Social introductions are based on gender (with deference being shown to the woman) while business introductions are based on rank. The exception to the hard and fast rules of both social and business protocol occurs when introductions involve members of the clergy, ambassadors, chiefs of state, and royalty. In these instances, those officials are accorded the most respect and the woman should be introduced to them. For example, "Bishop Daniels, I'd like to introduce to you Dr. Madeline Moss."

Proper introductions always include first and last names. In addition, they often include the use of honorifics—those titles that indicate membership in professional areas or marital status. Examples are Dr., Mr., Mrs., Miss, Professor, President, Judge, Ambassador, etc. Titles such as Senator, General, and Judge are for life. You may choose to omit the honorific when making an introduction but not the first and last names. If you use an honorific for one person, it is good manners to use an honorific for the other person involved in the introduction. For example, two people could be introduced correctly by saying either, "Judge Susie Sharp, I'd like to introduce to you Dr. Martha Roberts." Alternatively, you might introduce the two women by saying, "Susie Sharp, I'd like to introduce to you to Martha Roberts."

Address people in purely business settings the same way you address them in business/social settings. For example, if you call your boss "Mr." at the office, continue this habit even though the invitation you received referred to him by first name. Your spouse should address your boss and your boss' spouse with a title and last name if that is your usual business custom.

Add conversation bait to help people make conversation. Bait included in the introduction above might include information about the type of cases Judge Sharp hears, and the type of medicine Dr. Roberts practices, where each is from, their hobbies, or how the introducer knows each person.

A person introducing herself does not generally include her personal title but indicates a professional designation with conversation bait. For example, Dr. Roberts might introduce herself in the following way, "Hello, I'm Martha Roberts, an orthopedist from Atlanta." The correct reply would be, "Hello, Dr. Roberts. I'm Susie Sharp from Raleigh, NC, I'm holding court in this district." Dr. Roberts might choose to say, "Please call me Martha." Judge Sharp might choose to say, "Please call me Susie."

The mixing of the social and business worlds is inevitable, so it is smart to know the correct way to introduce people in a variety of settings and situations. But first, if you come upon a friend and a group of people you don't know, make the first move—introduce yourself.

Social Introductions

Introducing Yourself

Stand up. Look the person in his eyes, extend your hand for a firm web-to-web handshake, say your first and last names and something about yourself. For example, "Hello, I'm Jane Hight McMurry from Wilmington, NC, the keynote speaker for the convention."

Make each person feel important by providing important information about each person as you make the introduction. Disclosing the interests, special talents, hometowns or even the schools of the people being introduced will give a basis for small talk. For example, "Marie, I'd like to introduce you to my friend from the Swiss Bank office in Zurich, Terri Haywood. Terri is a former Olympic alpine skier and has a fun hobby—magic!" An introduction such as this can result in several avenues of conversation—the Olympics, skiing, Switzerland, banking, and magic.

Five Rules for Making Proper Social Introductions

1) *Introduce less important persons to more important persons.*

   Say the older, more important, or female's name first followed by one of the following phrases: "I'd like to present to you," "I would like to introduce to you," "I would like for you to meet," or simply, "this is" followed by the name of the person being introduced. For example, "Governor Goodman, I'd like to introduce to you Gordon Upshaw who is a new graduate from MIT. He is a software designer now living in Chicago."

2) *Introduce a man to a woman.*

   Introduce a man to a woman when they are the same age. Do this by first saying the woman's name. For example, "Sarah Lewtas, I'd like to introduce to you my friend, George Harris, a radio host and author from Sarasota. George, Sarah is a chef from Seattle."

3) *Introduce a younger person to an older person.*

   Do this by first saying the older person's name. Use the honorific to show respect. For example, "Mrs. Allen, I'd like to introduce to you my neighbor from Henderson, Barbara Maloy. Barbara, this is Mrs. Allen. Our fathers were friends in Vance County."

4) *Introduce a new friend to a group.*

   Do this by first saying the new friend's name. For example, "Eleanor Wilkins, I'd like you to meet my friends." Stand up and say the names of the

members in the group or have your friends introduce themselves to your friend.

5) *Introduce a nonfamily member to a family member.*
The other person is given precedence—except a
child who introduces a mother or father.

Business Introductions

Three Rules for Making Proper Business Introductions

1) *Introduce a junior member to a senior member of the
same company.*
Do this by saying the senior member's name first.

2) *Introduce a person from your own company to a
person outside of the company* even if the person
from your own company is the CEO. A client or
future client is always shown deference.

3) *Provide information to make conversation easy.*
For example, mention the interests, special talents,
hometowns or even the schools of the people being
introduced. This will give a basis for small talk. For
example, "Dorothea Bitler, I'd like to introduce to
you my friend from university, Edmond Talley who is
a wildlife editor from Montreal, Canada." An introduction such as this can result in several avenues of
conversation—wildlife, writing, university, the city
of Montreal and the country of Canada!

A fool proof method for making both business and
social introductions correctly is to use the following

formula: Say the name of the person accorded the most respect first, followed by the phrase "to you," followed by the name of the person being introduced. Just remember, flubbing up is forgivable, failing to make the introduction is not.

Responding to Introductions

- Do not reply with a simple "Hi" or "Hello."
- Stand up, extend your hand, smile, lean towards the person and say, "Hello ____. How do you do?" Some people prefer to say the phrase, "It's nice to meet you." The traditional response is "How do you do?" It's helpful if you can personalize what you say.
- Always repeat the person's name.
- Immediately ask the person to repeat a name if you didn't hear the name clearly or are not sure how to pronounce it.

Techniques for Remembering Names

Make a concerted effort to remember the names of people you meet. Do this by first paying attention to the new name when it is said during the introduction. Listen carefully to the name and if you do not hear it clearly ask the person to repeat the name. It is helpful to ask for the spelling of a unique sounding name. For example, you might say, "Hello, Dr. Loughlin. Do you spell your name L-o-c-k-l-i-n-g?" This will provide another opportunity for the brain to remember the name when the correct spelling is given.

Repeat the name aloud in your first response to the introduction as illustrated above and during the conversation. In addition, repeating the name silently will assist with remembering the name.

Other techniques that are helpful in remembering names are thinking of someone else you know with the same name or remembering the name with a word association. For example, a person might remember the name of a woman named Mrs. Strause by associating her name with the strawberry printed dress she is wearing. This system is not without danger. Someone I once knew used this technique when he met Mrs. Strause wearing her strawberry print dress and two months later greeted her saying, "Hello Mrs. Strawberry." Perhaps he would have had better luck if he had associated her by imagining straws coming out or her ears, but then there is the possibility of saying, "Hello Mrs. Hay" if one is not careful with the association.

At some point, everyone forgets a name. It is possible to let the person know that you remember him even when you admit that you have forgotten his name and ask for it again. Begin the conversation by reintroducing yourself to the person whose name you have temporarily forgotten. For example, "Hello, I'm Jane Hight McMurry. I believe we met at the technical conference in California." More often than not, the person will be grateful as he too may have forgotten a name and will readily supply his name. If the person does not reply with his name after I have refreshed his memory, I say, "Please tell me your name again" or "I really want to remember your name. Would you please repeat it?" Asking for the person's name again demonstrates interest in the individual and shows that you are human.

Conversations

> *The wit of conversation consists more in finding it in others than in showing a great deal yourself. He who goes from your conversation pleased with himself and his own wit, is perfectly well pleased with you.*
>
> *–Seventeenth-century French Moralist Jean de La Bruyère*

Business people who have good conversational skills are more likely to succeed even though they may not be better educated, smarter, or better looking. Studies conducted as early as the 1930s by the Carnegie Institute of Technology have revealed that in all fields only 15% of one's financial success in life is due to technical knowledge, while "skill in human engineering" (skill in communicating with people) is the factor responsible for the remaining 85% of financial success. John D. Rockefeller knew this. He said, "The ability to get along with people is as purchasable a commodity as sugar and coffee, and I pay more for that ability than any under the sun." He knew that the marketplace is fiercely competitive and that product knowledge and hard work are not enough to win clients and new contracts—or even keep the ones a business has. To outclass the competition and exceed bottom line goals often requires an essential business tool not found in every company. Rockefeller's success and the success of the business he ran were the results of individuals with excellent people skills.

A recent study conducted by The United States Census Bureau of Hiring and Training Management Practices was accomplished by surveying 3000 employers throughout the United States. The employers were asked to identify the top two skills sought in hiring new people. The survey required ranking in order of importance: previous work experience, recommendations by previous employers, positive attitude, experience in occupational field, good communication skills, and degree of education. The top two skills determined by this survey were a positive attitude and good communication skills. Research now indicates that up to 90% of your success in life is due to your people skills. Fortunately, people skills can be learned.

Mixing and mingling at the highest level is easy with a little advance preparation. The five Ps we talked about earlier will help you navigate conversations like a pro. "Prior Planning" ensures conversation success.

Plan for success by positioning yourself around people who can make a difference in your life. Do this often. Wake up every morning and ask yourself, "Who can I meet today who will make a difference in my success?" In fact, go a step further, write it in big, bold letters and tape it on your bathroom mirror.

Also consider: Who can help me meet my goals? Is it a prospective customer? A client? A colleague with contacts? An association with key members who may become prospects?

Don't settle interacting with the people who are the easiest to access. You need to reach outside your comfort zone where you will find new connections that will help you get what you want, need, and deserve.

When I was a young woman, I moved a thousand miles from my home in Chapel Hill, North Carolina to Hanover, New Hampshire where my former husband accepted a surgical residency. I knew no one in my new town. Lucky for me that the woman, Linda Nicks, who had lived in the house we moved into knew how to help me navigate my new jungle. In addition to the fresh flowers she'd picked from the meadow behind our house which she left on the mantel above our fireplace, she left an important list of people in the community who could help me. Beside their names and telephone numbers, she'd written short notes about each person. For example, next to Ron Fullington's name she wrote that he had a snow plow, would plow our driveway, was handy at fixing just about anything, and had a wife named Sandy and a daughter named Lisa who sewed, cleaned, etc. It made it easy for me to call Ron to introduce myself. I had a place to begin conversation.

Years later, I moved back to North Carolina. As fate would have it, Linda Nicks who had no ties to the South had moved to the same new town to which I moved! She brought me cookies and invited me to the opening of the local hospital's Hospitality House where I would meet new people in my new jungle. This time instead of giving me a handwritten list to help me navigate my new jungle, she personally prepared me for the people I would meet and then introduced me to them. Here's what she did.

Linda picked me up early in order to get a parking space smack dab in front of the Hospitality House. As people entered the building, she told me a little about each person as he or she entered. When we finally went inside, I found mingling easy and fun. I remember many people from that day, but I especially remember what my friend told me about Maryann Robison. "That woman can move mountains." Maryann could get things done in our community better than anyone else not only because she was nice to everyone, but because she was a pro at navigating the community to accomplish her goals. Maryann's daughter-in-law, Margaret, now carries the torch raising huge sums of money for good causes, primarily the result of her stellar skills at navigating the local business jungle.

It is perfectly all right to ask the person planning an event you will attend for a copy of the guest list. Event coordinators have the list and are usually happy to share it—after all, your knowing who will be attending will make you a better guest!

I visited an exclusive golf club whose members are from throughout the United States. On Friday evenings the club offers a popular event called "The Gathering" for members to gather for fellowship, cocktails, and an elegant buffet supper. After a round of golf at the club, my friend went into the secretary's office and asked for a printed list of the names of people with reservations who would be attending the evening's "Gathering." The secretary obliged. We took the list back to my friend's home. My friend mixed me a drink, got his membership book from a drawer, sat down in a rocking chair beside me on his porch overlooking the 6th green and went over the list telling me about each person who would be attending—name, city where each member was from, spouse's name, etc. He'd written notes in the book including information he'd learned about the members during previous rounds of golf and social activities. His review of the list was good for both of us. He refreshed his memory in preparation for follow-up on previous conversations and was prepared with conversation to introduce me to members with assurance that I was equipped with ideas for conversation with new partners. "Prior preparation prevents poor performance."

Do what you can to learn about people before you meet. One of my daughters recently was invited to a dinner party at the home of Barbara and Jack Nicklaus in Palm Beach Gardens, Florida. She was the date of a guest and assumed that the Nicklauses would only know her date. Win shares the following about the Nicklaus' ability to navigate the jungle as well as their ability to make others welcome in theirs.

I had the pleasure to be a guest at the Nicklaus' home. I would estimate there were at least 100 people in attendance, and everyone who came through the door was greeted in a receiving line first by Barbara and then by Jack. It was the perfect way for them to welcome their guests and they couldn't have been more gracious.

Barbara and Jack had done their homework on everyone who walked through the door. While I'm sure they did know many of those visiting their home that day, they took the time to learn about those they did not. It was my first time meeting them, but Barbara immediately made me feel welcome by conversing with me about my life in a way that showed she had taken her time to research and learn about me. Pretty spectacular.

You can tame your jungle like Barbara and Jack. Ensure the interest of your potential conversational partner by learning enough about his or her background, interests, and occupation so that you can intelligently discuss subjects which are important to him or her. Know some of the insider lingo particular to their interests and business. For example, a speaker planning a conversational encounter with a sports fan and an alumnae of the University of North Carolina at Chapel Hill during basketball season could easily learn what she needs from the sports page of a regional newspaper. She could discover the names of key players and easily figure out that the Carolina team is referred to as "The Tar Heels." In addition, she could read about important rivalries or hot issues that are on the minds of fans. Good conversation is enhanced by the introduction of topics that kindle the conversational bonfire.

Read at least one newspaper a day so you can initiate or participate in current event discussions. Survey every section—sports, leisure, international, entertainment, travel, and business. Even a cursory glance at the different sections will be of use to you later as you converse with people you do not know. Take time to periodically digest each section and to become aware of the vocabulary particular to different topics.

Read at least one book from *The New York Times* Best Seller List. Read reviews for all of them. As Louis Pasteur said, "Chance favors the prepared mind." Your memory will help you with conversation when you prepare in advance with diverse reading and experiences.

Prepare for conversation with people you have never met by consciously sampling a variety of activities and entertainments in your leisure. The vocabulary you pick up from a onetime experience (scuba diving, horseback riding, and going to the opera) can serendipitously provide the responsive cord that connects you to a new business associate.

Read the trade journals of potential conversation partners who function in a particular industry. These journals will help you to identify the hot issues concerning the industry as well as supply you with the vocabulary you need to sound like an insider.

If all else fails, use Eleanor Roosevelt's technique. Eleanor Roosevelt had a reputation for being able to talk to everyone including the most challenging conversation partners. A reporter once asked her how she always seemed to be able to talk to anyone. She said, "Sometimes I have to use the alphabet."

The startled reporter asked her to explain.

"Well, I start with the letter 'A.' For example, I might say, 'Nice crop of apples this year. What is your favorite variety of apple?' I never give up on anyone even if I have to go through the whole alphabet. One time I got all the way to the letter 'T.'"

Follow up on the last conversation you had with guests. For example, "You were planning a trip to Africa the last time I saw you. Tell me about the part of your trip that was the most exciting?" Ask open-ended questions that require more than a simple yes or no response.

Use clear language that focuses on the message you want to convey. Don't pad your message with "warm and fuzzy" words or expressions such as "I feel really good about so and so." Powerful women use powerful speech. Stick to the facts, get to the point, and leave out stories about other people that are gossip. Engaging in gossip will sabotage your career. Remember Joe Friday on the TV series *Dragnet?* "Just the facts ma'am. Just the facts."

You risk not getting what you want if you sugar coat or beat around the bush to get what you want. For example, if you are cold and you would like someone to turn up the thermostat, you will more likely get the desired result if you say, "I'm cold. Would you please turn up the thermostat?" than if you say, "It's cold in here."

Tone is important to get what you want. You must be loud enough to be heard and to receive the attention you need to get what you want.

Don't make statements that sound like questions. Speak with conviction. Record a conversation you have with another person. You may be surprised to hear an upward lilt at the end of your statements. Many women do this. Being aware of your voice will help you to correct many vocal issues. Hire a speech coach if you have trouble making progress.

Powerful women are polite but they are also smart and they know how to interact with all of the animals in the kingdom. Notice the first syllable of the word kingdom is king. Kings are men. Powerful women realize that to rule beside and not under kings they must do what men often do when they speak—be sure to say what they must when they must.

Polite people are taught not to interrupt but one of the most powerful women in American politics, former Secretary of State Madeline Albright, claims that learning to interrupt is one of the most important skills young women can learn. Research of Pat Heim and Susan Golant in their book, *Hardball for Women: Winning at the Game of Business,* confirms it. They found that men make 98% of all interruptions during mixed conversations to get what they want. How many opportunities have you missed because you failed to interrupt?

Speak up when you have something to say to get credit for your ideas. Not only will speaking first prevent others from saying what you are thinking first, it will also demonstrate your leadership, credibility and willingness to take risks.

Speak with confidence and do not give listeners an opportunity to discount your ideas by mentioning disclaimers such as "I'm no expert on xyz" or using the word "but." Some women make comments like this thinking that by putting themselves down they will appear less threatening without realizing that doing so is demeaning and shows lack of self-esteem. Powerful women who get what they want, need, and deserve do not denigrate themselves, their ideas, their thoughts, or their abilities.

Salary Negotiation

Women with equal education and technical skills continue to earn on average $.78 for every $1.00 a man earns. To prevent this and to facilitate getting what you want, it is helpful to negotiate. Prepare for negotiation by doing your homework and obtaining the information you need. It's important for you to be able to back up your request with facts. Facts persuade. Practice what you want to say before going into the situation. Winning lawyers do this and so should you. Be organized so you don't have to fumble looking for documents. Objections to your ideas will occur so anticipate how you will respond. Determine in advance what your bottom line is and what you are willing to give up. Listen, listen, listen. Ask open-ended questions to learn information that will help you reach an agreement.

Many women agree to whatever salary a company offers for their work. Companies are in business to make money. The less they pay you the more money they make. It's good business for them to try to get a good employee at the lowest possible cost. Be proactive in making sure the salary you accept is the best it can be.

Many women are taught that money is the root of all evil, that money is not important, and that it is not polite to talk about money. If you are one of these women, wake up and get over it. Financial fitness makes it possible to do what you want when YOU want.

You may not realize how much you are undercut until you negotiate. A company's first offer is rarely the maximum amount the business can actually afford to pay to have the best employees. It's up to you to convince your boss that paying you a little extra is worth it. What you should do is simple. *Ask.* You will be surprised that you will likely get a bigger paycheck if you ask.

Everything within a contract is negotiable. Your goal should be to get the money, the benefits, the vacation, the perks you deserve. Don't overlook appropriate requests for cell phones, automobiles, personal days, etc.

Five Magic Phrases Will Help You Get The Salary You Deserve

1. "That sounds a little low."

Keep it simple. No matter what figure is proposed, just state those five words and then close your mouth. Since no one can stand uncomfortable silences, your tight lips will force the employer to say something in response. Either he or she will make a new offer, ask you what you need, or tell you that's the best he can do.

Depending on the employer's response, use one of the following phrases.

2. "To make this job worth my time, I would need..."

This lets you take control of the situation. Be prepared with market research so you'll know what the job is worth. Two good sources to do wage checking for a job are www.salary.com and www.payscale.com. If you know how much the job should pay and factor in your experience and expertise, you should be able to determine how much you should be paid to do the job proposed. Make sure that you've done some research and that your figure is in the realm of what that particular job typically pays. Asking for a figure that's 20% more than the average payment is reasonable; asking for 200% more is not. Don't mince your words. State the amount and let your employer decide.

3. **"Considering the amount of work required to create develop, complete etc., can we agree to..."**
Consider the job the employer asked you to do. If it is developing/creating a product etc. that may be a perpetual money maker for your employer, and the contract you are offered asks for all rights or exclusivity in any way, use this as a bartering chip to ask for something more. You might ask for extra compensation for your creative talent that will bring the product or service to life or you might ask for delayed additional compensation that will be a percentage of realized earnings that are the result of your work.

4. **"I'm expecting more for this job."**
This simple statement puts the ball back in the employer's court. Again, follow this phrase with silence and allow the employer to come up with a new figure. This statement introduces the possibility that you could decide to work somewhere else if the employer doesn't meet your requirements.

5. "Can we work on that?"

This phrase shows the employer your interest in partnership. By using the word "we," you ask the employer to partner with you in coming up with more acceptable terms. This question opens the door to a variety of areas for improved compensation. You may choose to discuss salary, benefits, vacation, etc.

Remain professional in tone and demeanor. You must convey the impression that you are self-confident and aware of your value. If you don't value yourself, don't expect your employer or anyone else to value you.

As you navigate the jungle, avoid asking inappropriate personal questions. Instead, ask, "What do you enjoy doing in your free time?" Ask questions relevant to the occasion or the reason for the person's participation in the event you are both attending instead of talking about yourself, your own or the other person's health.

Off-color jokes are off-putting.

Giving too much information about anything—your children and grandchildren who may mean the world to you—is generally boring to others.

Avoid controversial topics like politics and religion. Use one of the following phrases to get your conversation back on a productive track when others bring up topics that are uncomfortable for you.

- "I'd like to suggest we change the subject."
- "This makes me uncomfortable."
- "Let's move on to other topics."
- "Let's agree to disagree."

Start conversations in business and social settings by using an indirect approach. Asking direct personal questions turns off potential business and social contacts as you are viewed as intrusive and nosy. Avoid questions such as: "Where do you live? What school did you attend? How do you know so and so? Where did you get...? How much did it cost? What church do you attend? Are you married? Do you have children? Who are you voting for?" Avoid asking, "What do your parents do?" This question is a turn-off because it makes the asker seem to be determining the value of the person. Do ask questions that focus on current topics of interest and subjects so broad that your questions will not be viewed as invasive.

The question, "What do you do?" is a question that is bothersome to many conversationalists. The risk of offending is most likely with two groups of people. First, people who are not proud of their jobs, and second, people who are not employed. The second category includes people who may be fortunate enough not to need to work and do not wish to discuss that privilege. Ask the question, "What do you do?" only when you sense that the individual will be amenable to answering it and that he will enjoy talking about his work. The best phrase to use when you are not sure is, "What do you enjoy doing?" The person who enjoys his work will gladly discuss his job and the person who does not work or like his job is free to direct conversation to whatever he likes best.

Try as hard as you like, you are human and will inevitably make an unintentional conversational blunder—something that hurts or upsets your conversational partner (CP). Your unintended comments are not intended to be insensitive, but for your CP the comment is uncomfortable and/or painful. You likely will be aware that you have uttered something you wish you had not as soon as you speak. You will likely recognize this because your CP may fall silent, snap back at you, or perhaps even tell you that your comments are not appropriate or that your comments are mean. The best way to rectify this is by addressing the blunder immediately. For example, "I'm sorry. I did not realize that would upset you." As an alternative you might say, "Please forgive me I feel terrible. I did not intend to hurt your feelings." Your CP will likely forgive you and appreciate your contrition if your apology is warm and sincere.

Read the body language of the key people you observe when you enter a room. Determine which key people are currently the easiest to approach. The person standing alone typically is feeling awkward and will appreciate your attention. Dyads with closed body language standing with their heads close together and their backs turned are generally more difficult to enter than triads. When you approach a group, stand on the fringe of the conversation space with one foot slightly forward if a small space is open. The participants will typically open the space to let you enter. Listen to the conversation to grasp the topic. Enter the group of people you do not know by waiting for a break in conversation and then coupling a self-introduction with a comment. For example, you might encounter a group discussing the upcoming

NCAA (National Collegiate Athletic Association) tournament. When a break occurs, you might say, "Hello, I'm Jane Hight McMurry. I was listening to ESPN radio on my way here and they reported that Duke's point guard fell during practice and is injured." Most groups welcome a new breath of conversational life.

Welcome newcomers to your conversational group by slightly opening the space between you and the group when you notice someone who wants to join your group.

Body language at every business and social affair should be professional. Remember, the only acceptable form of professional touch is the handshake. This is not the place to demonstrate romantic affection for anyone.

Make a goal to meet seven or eight people per hour. Average topics of small talk conversation take approximately eight minutes to exhaust. This does not mean avoiding your coworkers. Acknowledge them and include them in conversations.

Putting yourself in host mode will help you feel like you belong. Giving a sincere compliment or repeating a second-hand compliment that you've heard about the person is a good way to start a conversation.

Small Talk

There is no such thing as "small talk." It's the foundation for all "big talk." Use it to transition deeper by listening for clues.

Small talk conversation stagnates when cliché topics like the weather and food are exhausted. Sometimes the body language of conversational partners indicates a willingness to terminate or continue the conversation. If the body language is open, and the facial expression shows interest, the savvy conversationalist knows what to listen for and how to steer the conversation to deeper talk. Transitioning from small talk is easy for the good listener. He listens for a topical cue (a word or reference) to direct talk in a deeper direction. For instance, the good listener might hear his conversational partner say, "This food tastes like the food in France." The alert listener might pick up on the word France and respond, "Have you been to France? I've always wanted to travel there and sample the regional foods and wines." The conversation then begins to take on new life. Even though the person who asked the question about France may not have a deep interest in France, chances are good that the conversational partner does and for that person the small talk is no longer small.

The conversationalist transitioning from small talk to deeper conversation often reflects back to the speaker not only the words he has heard that reveal that he has a literal understanding of the message, but also words indicating an understanding of the feelings of the speaker. For example, the conversation about France may digress to conversation about a trip to a castle in the Loire Valley where the person took cooking classes given by a famous chef. "Wow, it must have been exciting to visit that special part of France. I can tell that you have more than a passing interest in good food," the attentive listener may empathetically respond. Using empathizers, (short, simple supportive statements), demonstrates understanding which is important in establishing rapport in a relationship so that conversation can continue beyond small talk. Listening for what is emotionally significant to the conversation partner and letting him know that you understand what is significant to him is more important than any clever remark you might venture to make. Why? Because in a new relationship people generally feel that the least interesting things about themselves are more important than the most fascinating things about people they do not know.

Use phrases like, "I can understand why you feel..." "I can see you really understand..." "I appreciate why you..." "It's obvious you really worked hard for..." (Note: these phrases are also useful in relationships that have developed and become meaningful. These same empathizers then demonstrate sincere interest in the other person which may be greater than the interest in one's self.) The use of the pronoun "you" can be used positively to effectively shift the focus of the conversation onto the other person. Remember, people subconsciously perceive themselves as more important than any other person, place, or thing.

One further tip, respect your conversational partner by waiting until after he has had the pleasure of sharing his experience before you interrupt or add that you also have been there, done that, etc. Later, if your conversational partner asks why you didn't tell him earlier, you can further increase his appreciation of you with a statement such as, "I was enjoying hearing your description so much..."

Developing and Maintaining Conversations and the Use of Subliminal Rapport Building Techniques

Conversations typically begin with clichés and later move on to a phase which may include the introduction of facts. As rapport increases, feelings become a feature of the dialogue. Later as conversation grows deeper, conversations that are more intimate are characterized by the use of "we" and "us" as experiences are shared between conversational partners.

Good conversationalists match the mood of the people with whom they converse. This rapport establishing technique puts the conversational partner at ease. Jovial, tranquil, enthusiastic moods which are matched make the conversational partner feel that the person he is speaking with is in step with him.

It has been said that the prettiest sound in the whole world is the sound of one's own name. Use the name of the person with whom you are speaking, but avoid overusing it so you will not sound as if you are patronizing the person. If you cannot remember the person's name, ask the person to repeat it. Say something like, "I really want to remember your name. Will you please repeat it?" This will show that you care enough about the person to remember who they are so don't hesitate to ask. Use your conversational partner's name effectively by looking the person in the eye when there is a break in the conversation. Lean slightly forward. Enthusiastically ask a question that requires thought to answer with more than a simple yes or no.

A technique called captioning is the excerpting of a phrase or story from a previous conversation and relating it in some way back to the current conversation. The meaning of the caption is understood only by the two people making captioning function somewhat like a private language between communicators. It establishes a bond between communicators that is unique and gives the feeling of history to a relationship even though the relationship is new. Many business people will make a new acquaintance feel like an old friend by finding something in a previous conversation that the conversational partner liked which they highlight in a later conversation. Captioning may even take the form of a private joke between two people. Caption something positive that you and your conversational partner shared.

The use of nicknames is another technique that is sometimes effective in establishing a strong subliminal bond, thus transitioning acquaintances into friends. For example, two acquaintances paired in a golf game at a company retreat may give each other complimentary nicknames based on a round of golf. "The Eagle" or "Ms. Par" may arise. If you give someone a nickname, make sure that it is one the person likes.

Business people who feel comfortable may ask their conversational partner if he or she had a nickname growing up and then ask if they'd like to be called by that name. For instance, Allison may be asked if anybody ever called her "Alli." Perhaps it is the name her friends still call her and Allison responds that she would like her new friend to call her by that name. Allison may tell her new friends to call her "Alli" instead of Allison before they ask. The sharing and encouragement of the use of the nickname will likely accelerate the feeling of being a friend from that of being an acquaintance.

Two of my favorite nicknames belonged to my father and to his first cousin whose names were Henry and James. I could always tell who their closest friends were because those people called them "Pat" and "Chunka." My father's nickname was given to him by school friends when he was a young boy and recited Patrick Henry's address for a school assembly. James was an excellent baseball player who could really "chunk" the ball and was dubbed "Chunka" by his teammates when he was a young baseball player.

Divulging information is a technique requiring the sharing of privileged information. It may be in the form of a secret or confession which illustrates vulnerability and indicates need of help or protection. The divulged information may be confidential information given in hopes of making the new acquaintance feel special. Although the technique of divulging information some-times may be useful, it usually backfires as the person receiving the confidential information often becomes suspicious and curious to learn why the confidential information was shared so early in a relationship. Further, it could make him wonder what other personal or business information the person may be harboring.

Some business people seek to establish rapport by mirroring nonverbal and verbal language. They may mimic their conversational partner's body language including posture, stance, walk, etc. This produces subliminal rapport. In addition, they match the perceived mood of the speaker which may seem happy, enthusiastic, pensive, or sad. On succeeding encounters, the person seeking to further establish rapport may dress in clothes similar to the person's clothing with whom he is trying to develop a friendship.

Mirroring may extend to echoing the use of verbal language, including the copying of voice and diction. It is important to understand that every communicator uses speech in a way that can signal much about his education as well as socioeconomic status. Every communicator subliminally perceives his conversational partner as similar or different from himself based on speech. When the businessperson actively listens to his conversational partner's speech, he can discern the grammatical patterns, word choices, and/or accents that he may wish to adopt in order to match the new conversational partner's style, thereby establishing rapport and minimizing differences. Sales presentations often seem to be more successful when conversational partners "speak the same language." People feel a sense of connection when they hear their own words echoed back to them. Using terms common to the conversational partner's makes the speaker sound in tune with him, thus increasing the likelihood of mutual understanding. Blending seems to enhance the communication process. I am not advocating that the businessperson change nonverbal and verbal patterns. I am suggesting that the businessperson learn to flex style to establish rapport and to encourage the smooth dealing of business in order to achieve what is wanted, needed, and deserved.

You can further promote subliminal rapport by using a subtle technique involving reflecting back conversation that indicates sensory understanding. Effective business communicators can do what neurolinguists do to identify the primary sense datum used by a speaker. People rely on the five senses (sight, hearing, smell, taste, and touch) to interpret information as they sift through the many elements which contribute to a message. People talk about the world in terms of the senses they use to interpret their world, usually employing one dominant sense as a means of personal perception of the world. Listen for the use of phrases which contain words pertaining to the senses to determine how your conversational partner interprets the world. Listed below are the five senses accompanied by samples of phrases used by speakers who interpret the world using a particular sense.

Visually Oriented: "I see what you mean." "That looks great to me." "The way I see it is…"

Auditory Oriented: "What I hear you saying…" "That sounds good to me." "The news was music to my ears."

Kinesthetic (Touch) Oriented: "I feel uneasy about that." "I've got a gut feeling about that." "I was touched by his remarks." "The project manager's appeal moved me."

Smell Oriented: "That deal smells fishy." "Smell the roses." "I smell a rat." "He can smell a buck from a hundred miles away."

Taste Oriented: "Transacting that deal was sweet." "I don't have a taste for doing business with that company." "Their method of advertising leaves a bad taste in my mouth." "The sugar coated version of the deal was just too much for me." "His acid remarks were noted by me." "He seasoned the deal by ..." "The president's salty remarks..."

Another excellent way to increase subliminal rapport with a conversational partner is to use words relevant to the conversational partner's business and personal life. Know the trade terms used in the person's profession as well as the terms the person knows through activities away from work. This technique is powerful and requires knowledge about the conversational partner's lifestyle and interests. It subliminally makes your communication partner aware that you think like him and share his interests. For example, consider the rapport a pharmaceutical representative can more quickly establish with an ear, nose, and throat doctor who is also a sports fan if he not only knows the correct medical lingo for the doctor's specialty, but also uses the words the doctor is fond of using and hearing away from his life in medicine. The pharmaceutical rep's small talk with the doctor at a medical meeting could easily burgeon into a discussion of a recently televised baseball game. On a subsequent visit to the surgeon's office, he could establish subliminal rapport by using sporting terms in a sales pitch. For instance, the pharmaceutical rep might say that the new medication will cover all the bases when used to treat otitis media. He has used the baseball lingo "covering all the bases" and the correct medical lingo in otorhinolaryngology for an earache "otitis media." Translation: the medicine will effectively treat fever, swelling, etc. (all the bases) in patients who have ear aches (otitis media). This technique is powerful and will make your business associate feel a strong connection with you. After all, you speak the same language.

The last rapport-establishing device involves the use of the pronoun "you" that makes it easy for the receiver to understand his role in the message. As stated earlier, people like to hear their own names spoken. They also like to easily understand what they need to understand when interpreting a message. The receiver understands the message in terms of "how does that affect me." The sender can facilitate the person's understanding of how it affects him by phrasing the message in terms of the second person. Perhaps you can most easily grasp this concept by using the example of the pharmaceutical representative conversing with the doctor. The pharmaceutical rep could choose to tell the doctor about the method of prescribing a new drug in one of two ways. First, using language that requires the doctor to make his own translation of how to prescribe the medicine, "The drug is administered three times per day with food." Alternatively, using language in which the translation has been made for him, "You tell the patient to take the medicine with meals every day." People respond more readily to that which they easily understand and the pronoun "you" facilitates their understanding.

This technique is one of the easiest and most effective of the subliminal rapport building techniques.

Gaining Control of Conversations

Powerful conversationalists are aware of the risks and communication breakdowns that can occur at any point in any conversation. They are willing to take that risk and do not hesitate to be the first to say "hello" and to introduce themselves, and to initiate topics of conversation. To gain control of a conversation you must be open, friendly, and genuinely interested in every conversational partner. Further, you must be open to new ideas, topics, and people. Accept people as they are, not how people wish they were. When someone asks, "What's new?" be prepared to answer with more than a feeble, "Not much." "Nothing." "Same old thing." "Just working." Answer with topics you're interested in talking about because of who you are, where you've been, and what you're looking for. Responding with your ideas, recent successes, or questions about what you're looking for will turn your small talk into smart talk.

Asking open-ended questions will lead you to success. Open-ended questions are questions that require more than a yes or no response. For example, "Tell me about..." "What is the biggest challenge you face in your business?"

Beauty without brains is like a book without words.

—*Jane Hight McMurry*

Chapter Nine

Midnight at the Oasis:
The Rule of Three

The secret of getting ahead is getting started.

—*Sally Berge*

The easiest people to meet at any oasis are the wallflowers. They will welcome your attention! Initiate your meeting by opening with a neutral compliment to the person (nothing to do with physique or personal details), introducing yourself and asking how the person knows the host, or by asking a question such as, "Excuse me, what are you eating? It looks delicious…"

Showing interest in the individuals you meet by learning about their jobs, companies, interests—anything but the weather—will help you develop a personal relationship that can lead to a business relationship. Demonstrate your interest by giving feedback, nodding, paraphrasing, and SMILING!

When you enter an event for business purposes, have a networking goal of perhaps garnering three to five follow-up appointments. Clarify what you hope to learn and prepare two questions to get the information you seek. At large gatherings focus on real prospects like a systematic business call. Ask questions to determine valid prospects. Don't aimlessly walk around! Make others feel good and get people you meet to talk about themselves. It's okay to ask people how they happen to be attending the event. Put yourself in host mode. Act as if you belong and are thrilled to be included!

Start conversations with people you don't know by first introducing yourself, offering minimal conversation bait, and asking a question. For example, "Hello, I'm Jane Hight McMurry, one of the speakers at this convention. What are your roles at this convention?" People will generally respond by telling you their names and about their business roles. Do not talk about yourself and your business at the beginning of a conversation with a new person. You will appear to come on too strong. Do ask questions that are relevant to the occasion or the reason for the other person's participation in the event. Show interest in the individual, his job, and his company. Foster conversation in that direction instead of bringing up topics like sports, the weather, or entertainment that will not lead to sharing information that will lead to business. Conversation starters include:

- "What's been your best day at work this year?"
- "What was the best session you went to today and why did you like it?"
- "What stories do people tell about the great leaders/milestones in this organization?"

- "Who's been your role model or mentor here?"
- "What are you looking forward to?"

People will likely begin to ask you about your business and then you can feel comfortable sharing information about yourself and your company that might lead to future business deals. Keep your conversation about yourself and your business brief. You might offer that you'd love to send them some information about your business and that perhaps you could exchange business cards for this purpose. This will give you a reason to follow up your conversation in writing. Remember, you want to move on about every eight minutes.

Good conversation is like a good game of tennis with the verbal exchange going back and forth between partners. Return the conversation back to the other person. The game of conversation, like the game of tennis, is no fun if it is one-sided.

Be first to show interest in others, but when asked about yourself, remember the following *Rule of Three.*

Rule of Three

Rule One. Reveal in the first three seconds what you do in six to ten words. For example when people ask me what I do, I say, "I teach people how to get what they want, need, and deserve."

Rule Two. When you have thirty seconds and your conversation partner asks, "How do you do that?"

or if he says, "Tell me more," tell him in thirty seconds who your customers are, what makes you unique, and how you help. Don't go too deep—you're networking for later! Here's what I say, "I do professional speaking and conduct training, workshops, and seminars. I customize for groups. I love music and The Beatles so my presentations often include music—especially The Beatles." (notice bait)

Rule Three. If the listener is still interested, use three minutes more to ask your conversation partner about his business. I say, "Tell me about your business." Depending on what I learn about my conversation partner's need for leadership, teamwork, customer service, or information helpful to women, I continue my conversation as follows.

"I present a *'Ticket to Ride'* series of programs using stories and music of The Beatles to equip business people with interpersonal skills."

If my conversation partner is a woman who belongs to a women's group, I say, "I present a popular program customized for women called *'Navigating the Lipstick Jungle: Go from Plain Jane to Getting What You Want, Need, and Deserve'* that teaches women to politely and powerfully roar to get what they want, need, and deserve. I love working with women and have had fun customizing material that transforms their personal and professional lives."

Use thirty minutes or three hours more at a follow up meeting. When I'm at a networking event and the person wants more information, I say, "Thank you for interest. I'd love to learn more about you and your business. I would be happy to tell you more about how my programs help people be successful but I don't want to monopolize your time at this wonderful event. We're both here to enjoy connecting with lots of people and I don't want you to lose the chance to meet and visit with people you want to see. Let's continue our conversation when we can focus on each other. Would you like to meet for a cup of coffee later this week?"

Schedule a follow-up meeting so you won't jeopardize the present opportunity to continue networking. Exchange contact information.

It's generally best to suggest a neutral location to meet like a coffee shop so you won't seem pushy or like you are expecting a commitment. If you don't set a meeting, at least send a quick email or card saying how nice it was to meet them.

A good way to meet people you don't know is to use a team-up trick with a friend who is attending the same event. The team-up trick works this way. You and your friend separate after you have greeted the hosts and any honored guests. Circulate as previously discussed. Later walk over to the group your friend has become a part of and stand beside him or slightly back and to his side so he can see you. At a break in the conversation your friend should introduce you and offer information about you that will interest your new contacts. The most helpful part of this introduction is that you can each wow the group with accolades about each other that you would be uncomfortable saying about yourselves.

Disengage from the person or group you are speaking to by summing up your conversation, thanking the person, shaking hands, and moving on. To do this, extend your hand and say something like, "Brenda, I've enjoyed meeting you and hearing about your trip to London. Thank you for sharing your news and adventures. I hope we can get together soon." Smile and move on. If the person is a clinger, you might need to add, "Let's mingle a little now. I hope we see each other again before the event is over." The person you are leaving feels satisfied (you have demonstrated that you have listened by summing up the conversation), she feels positive (you have thanked her and shaken her hand), and you have indicated a desire to interact with her later. Further, she is now free to continue her networking unrestricted, whereas some conversational endings such as, "Excuse me, I am thirsty and need a drink," may be misinterpreted incorrectly in at least three ways. First, the person may expect your return; second, he may feel welcome to accompany you to the bar; or third, he may feel that you are bored with his company.

Some professionals disengage from conversation by saying something like, "I've enjoyed talking to you. Why don't we mingle a little?" or "Let's mingle a little now. I hope we see each other again before the party is over." I find this technique somewhat off-putting and prefer the more palatable first technique discussed.

You may find yourself conversing with someone who looks around the room instead of at you and appears uninterested in what you are saying. This conversational partner (CP) may make feeble attempts at conversation but you sense that your CP is not listening to you. In such instances, you have a couple of options. First, you can try focusing fully on your CP and considering the vast potential range of his needs. It may be that he is looking at the people gathered because he is worried that he may miss something or perhaps he is searching the room for a special person. On the other hand, it could be that he becomes nervous when speaking with anyone at any length. You may finally consider that he is simply not interested in talking with you and has not learned to gracefully disengage in a conversation. The onus is on you to terminate the conversation as tactfully as possible and move on. Do this by taking advantage of a pause in conversation (the sooner the better) and disengaging as we discussed earlier by smiling, summing up your conversation, thanking the person, shaking hands and moving on.

Speaking of pauses, one of the most effective elements of strong communication is actually nothing at all—a pause! Power business communicators use pauses that last three to four seconds to let the import of their message sink in, to create drama, and to command attention. Instead of using non-words, say nothing at all. A silent pause has a powerful effect.

Business Cards

Carry an ample supply of fresh business or social cards when you plan to gather at any oasis. Business cards offer the name of your business, business address, telephone numbers, e-mail address, and/or anything else relevant for locating you in regards to business life. Social cards contain only your name and social contact information—usually a personal telephone number and address. Your cards reflect your quality. A neat professional appearance with current information is important. Do not write on your cards to correct information that has changed. Immediately print new cards with correct information.

Do not pass your cards out liberally like candy. It will make your card seem like it is not important. Look for a reason to hand out your business card. As you listen, think about the resources you have, or the contacts you have that would be of interest or help to the other person. Listening will provide you with the reason to ask the person you are with for his card and to offer him your card. For example, "I just read a wonderful article about that. I'll send it to you." or, "My friend Katherine works with international importers. I'll be glad to put you in touch with her."

When someone offers you information, you have the perfect opportunity to say, "Thank you so much for sending me the information. Here's my card." However, if you are with a significantly higher-ranking businessperson, it is appropriate to wait for him or her to ask to exchange cards.

Correctly use cards. Present your business card with the print facing the person. Business cards are frequently exchanged during business introductions and are expected to be presented during business introductions in some cultures. Accept a business card as you would a gift. Nod with thanks and understanding as you accept another person's card and take a moment to study it. Ask questions to show your interest about information you learn from the card. Do not fold or write on the other person's card in his presence. If you want to make notes about the person, wait until you are in a private place. Place the new card in your case or other appropriate place that shows respect of the card to the person who gave it to you. For example, do not place the card in your hip pocket where you will sit on it.

Carry cards in a case that conveys the image you want. Some cases have separated pockets for incoming and outgoing cards. Make sure you have some system for making sure you do not mistakenly hand out another person's card.

Never exchange business cards publicly if the event you are attending is a predominantly social occasion such as a wedding or small dinner in a private home. Use discretion if you want to exchange business cards at social events.

Know the business card protocol of your international business partner's culture. Business cards are an important device for establishing and maintaining international contact. In China and Japan, it is expected that business cards will be presented during business introductions and received with both hands, thumbs on the upper corners of the card so the card will be easily readable by the recipient. However, in the Middle East and some parts of Asia, the business card is presented with only the right hand because the left hand is used for bodily hygiene and considered unclean.

Do print your information in the language of the people you are likely to meet. Include your title as in some cultures the title is interpreted as an extension of the person who has given it. Print your card on high quality white or beige paper (other colors may work depending on your profession) with black ink. Your card is the tangible representation of you that others will use to remember you.

Be Memorable

To be remembered requires repetition. You can't say or do something once and leave it at that. Successful business people say what they want as many times as they need until they get the desired response. Would you remember a commercial if you only saw it once? Consumers repeatedly exposed to messages eventually buy the products, services etc., they remember due to repetition.

You also have to make multiple impressions on those you are networking with in order to build brand awareness. Repetition is in direct connection with positioning. Once you find people with whom to network, reach out and find hundreds more who can help you reach your goals.

Be three things to people you meet—valuable, courteous, and smart. *Be valuable* by following up with people you've met based on their needs that you've learned about through listening. Email, phone, share articles/information, or send invitations for coffee, lunch, golf etc., within two business days following your event because people will still remember you. *Be courteous* by sending a thank you note. *Be smart* by recording contact information and memory joggers about people in your database so you can help others when you have a reason to help them!

Do not steal, swear, beg or lie.
But if you must steal...steal away from bad company.
If you must swear, swear to tell the truth.
If you must beg, beg someone's pardon
if you've done them wrong.
If you must lie, lie in a good person's arms.
                              —*A mother's advice to her daughter*

Chapter Ten

Deadly Sins:
Faux Pas That Can Cost Big Game

Mistakes are part of the dues one pays for a full life.

—Sophia Loren

Deadly conversation sins include interrupting, finishing the other person's sentences, saying that you have already heard the story or joke being told, criticizing, appearing bored, and correcting trivial facts that always embarrass the person being corrected. People simply will find you arrogant, boorish, and insensitive. The person who corrects others in public over trifling matters is the biggest loser of all. This person is killing not only her personal relationship but also her business relationship as her insensitivity to others marks her as a person insensitive to everyone. Be kind, show interest, and ask non-invasive questions.

A friend told me a story about a young girl who had a terrible temper. Her parents knew her temper would cause her trouble in life. No matter how much they pleaded with their daughter, she continued to lose her temper.

Her father had an idea. One day after an unpleasant hissy fit, he decided rather than to scold his daughter, he would give her a present. To the girl's surprise, the gift was a bag full of nails.

"What are these for?" the puzzled girl asked her father.

"Every time you lose your temper, you must go into the backyard and hammer a nail into the back of the fence."

The girl lost her temper many times and by the end of the first day had hammered twenty-nine nails into the fence. Her arm began to ache. She began to control her anger and by the end of the second month the number of hammered nails dwindled to only one a day.

The day finally arrived when the girl did not lose her temper a single time. She had discovered it was easier to hold her temper than to hold a hammer and pound nails into the fence. She excitedly ran to her father and beamed as she announced, "Dad, I didn't have to hit one nail today!" Her father congratulated her. He then told his daughter that as a reward she was to remove one nail for each day that she was able to control her temper.

Two more months passed. The girl went to her father and with even more pride than before announced that all the nails were removed.

The father took his daughter by the hand and walked with her to the fence. He observed the fence and said, "You have worked hard, but look at the holes in the fence. The fence will never be the same. When you say and do things in anger, your words and actions leave scars that will remain forever." Looking his daughter straight into her eyes, the girl's father made sure that the young girl received a lasting lesson when he said, "Always remember that a verbal wound is as painful as a physical one."

Stop and reflect on the words you use and the ways you use them. How do you use words? If you use words to gossip, ridicule, spread rumors, mock and demean others, you leave holes in the fences of other people's hearts and without even knowing it, leave massive holes in your own heart. Think before you speak.

When you affirm, support, forgive, enable and redeem others it helps to heal the holes you have created or those that have been created in you. You can leave either holes or healing as a legacy in your world. Choose words to build up and not to destroy.

The first conversational faux pas you want to avoid is saying anything detrimental or harmful about anyone. You will be the one who looks bad. People who talk badly about others get a reputation for being negative and tend to be avoided because listeners fear that they will be the next target of the person who speaks ill of others.

The second conversational faux pas is giving unwanted advice. Few people want advice even when they ask for it. People who give advice sound like teachers or parents so save giving advice for times when you are in one of those roles.

The third conversational faux pas is talk about money, such as how much things costs, and love—yours or anyone else's. These private topics make others feel uncomfortable so save this conversation for your most intimate relationships.

Tone is important to get what you want. You must be loud enough to be heard and to receive the attention you need to get what you want.

DO NOT CHEW GUM IN PUBLIC. Chewing gum will make you look like you have the sense of a four-legged water buffalo.

Alcohol ruins careers *and lives.* You may think you have the power to hold your liquor and remain dignified when you drink but one sip too many can cause you to lose your dignity and self-control. People who compromise self-control compromise business. Don't let after hours behavior sabotage what you work hard to achieve by day. Illegal substances are just that. If you're caught, you can lose your job and forfeit getting what you want, need, and deserve.

Chapter Eleven

True Grit in the Jungle:
The Power of Polite

*Life is not so short but that there is
always time for courtesy.*

—Ralph Waldo Emerson

B e powerfully polite in the jungle. Manners are the grit that will set you apart from the herd. It's baloney that nice girls don't get the corner office. Nice women do because good manners and etiquette are liberating. They free you from thinking about yourself so you can focus on other people. The people you work with will be more productive, loyal, and willing to follow your lead. People will choose to do business with you. When products and services are equal, people choose to do business with people who treat them with courtesy and respect. They will even pay more to do business with you! Brush up on your Ps&Qs. Read an etiquette book. *The Etiquette Advantage* and *The Dance Steps of Life* are straightforward, easy to read, and what I call "Lipstick 101." Manners and etiquette are the foundation for communication that will get you what you want.

Be nice to people. Smile. Most people you meet are hurting about something whether they are rich or poor, smiling or frowning. Your smile and your kind words can mean more than you can imagine. It costs nothing to be nice to people and it means more than any gift that costs money. Emerson wrote, "Kindness is one of the most beautiful compensations in life. We can never help another without helping ourselves."

Show respect to everyone. You may have more education, a greater breadth of experience, a more illustrious family tree, and deeper pockets than the people you work with, but you are no better than anyone else. Show respect for every human being you meet.

Thanking people is important. In business, it's not just who you know, but who you thank. An important way to strengthen your business relationships is by showing appreciation to everyone who is valuable to you. Everyone likes to feel appreciated. It is important to thank the people who do business with you, as well as everyone in your life who is helpful to you.

There are no "little people." Thanking support personnel is important. Most employees don't mention their pay or other perks when asked what motivates them to perform at their highest level. What they do mention is that they are more willing to work hard when they know they are appreciated. Showing appreciation to your staff for their efforts improves their performance which in turn is good for your business. Don't forget to show appreciation to the maintenance crew either—they make your business look good. No one can read your mind. You must take action to let people know the value of their efforts to you. Silent gratitude is useless.

A powerful way you can be polite is to write a handwritten thank you note to the people who help you. The sooner you write it the stronger its impact—aim for within two business days after a courtesy is extended to you.

Black ink is most professional followed by blue ink. *Use your own personal paper*—not company letterhead. Company stationery is for correspondence that reflects company policy. Never use it for personal correspondence. Women can choose to write on a correspondence card, letter sheet, or a fold-over note often referred to as an informal note. (Traditional etiquette cautions men not to use informal notes which are a traditional paper for women). Avoid cute floral paper when thanking someone for anything connected to business. Choose quality to reflect the quality image you intend.

I once had a twenty-eight year old client who lost his job as a banker in New York City. His mother asked me if I would do a one-on-one coaching session with him to prepare him for upcoming interviews. During our coaching session, I discussed the importance of a handwritten note to thank people who would be interviewing him. He scoffed at my advice and adamantly refuted the idea saying, "No one in New York writes handwritten thank you notes. They email." I listened and then offered that perhaps that because no one else seemed to be writing handwritten notes in New York that he might want to consider writing a note to differentiate himself from his competition.

About three weeks later, my colleague from Boston conducted a business dining seminar in New York for the wealth management division of a well-known bank. When she arrived at the training site, the person who hired her led her into the room where the training would occur. He pointed to personalized boxes of William Arthur stationery positioned at the place setting of each banker who would attend the seminar. He said, "I know we didn't discuss thank you notes in the training you agreed to provide, but would you please explain to our bankers the importance of a handwritten note to our customers?"

The handwritten thank you note may be rare, but it is very much alive in New York among people who wield power and interact with the powerful.

A simple "thank you" doesn't require much, but the payoff of your tiny investment is that you will stand favorably apart from the rest of the pack. People choose to do business with people they favor when the services or products are equal.

Saying thank you is expected for invitations that cross over from business to social occasions such as family entertainments, dinner parties, cocktail buffets including a spouse or significant other, office parties, or events at which you are a guest. A verbal thank you to the host is sufficient when you leave events such as an office party at a restaurant where you share a meal in the ordinary course of business. Some business people opt to reiterate their thanks for these routine business invitations in their next business correspondence instead of writing a separate thank you note.

Unexpected thank you notes make a great impression. Consider thanking people for their business and/ or for what they have done for you throughout the year at nontraditional times like Thanksgiving instead of Christmas. If you do send a printed greeting card, personally sign it. For even greater impact, add a short hand-written note of thanks to a printed card.

Thank people when they offer kind words about you or your business. Let them know you appreciate the positive feedback. They will also appreciate it when you take the time to recognize their accomplishments or good work.

Thank people for their support and advice. Take this opportunity to let the person know about your areas of expertise and willingness to be available should they need you.

Sign your professional notes with an appropriate closing that will not be misinterpreted. "Sincerely," "Yours truly," "Best regards," or "Warm regards" are safe choices. Omit any honorific due you, but do sign both your first and last names.

The well-written thank you note will mark you as a polished professional and will set you apart as one with savoir-faire. The best notes are personal, specific, brief and prompt. Personally thank the people to whom you owe gratitude, including the person who entertained you, or if you entertained, the support staff or others who helped make the affair run smoothly. Tell exactly what you appreciate and don't exaggerate or continue at length. Four to five well-written sentences are plenty. Be prompt, but if you can't be, remember it is never too late to say thank you or to send a note of appreciation.

A follow-up telephone thank you the next day is nice, the e-mail or faxed thank you is better than nothing, but the handwritten note is by far the most appreciated and effective means of saying thank you. The handwritten note demonstrates the personal touch–something that is often lacking in business and therefore highly prized. The old Crane Stationary advertisement said it best, "To the best of our knowledge, no one ever cherished a fax."

The advantage an emailed thank you has over a handwritten note is its ability to be sent as a copy and forwarded to others for public recognition of a job well done. A sample of an email note of thanks appropriate for distribution to everyone in a department might read as follows.

Dear Alston,

Thank you for all the great work on the Ellison project! As you know, this was a really important project for our company and it is thanks to you that the project was completed on time.

Everyone on the team appreciates and applauds your work!

Best regards,
Kiernan

Show appreciation whenever and wherever you can. A campaign to thank military service people was started by Scott Truitt. It is a simple and easy way to thank military men and women you do not know without having to approach them. Here are the steps to the Gratitude Campaign thank you sign.

- Place your hand over your heart like you do when you say the Pledge of Allegiance.

- Pull your hand down and out.

- Bend at the elbow and do not bend your wrist.

- Stop around your belly button with your hand flat, palm up and angled towards the military service person you are thanking.

Technology... is a queer thing.
It brings you great gifts with one hand,
and it stabs you in the back with the other.

—*Carrie P. Snow*

Chapter Twelve

Jungle Music:
Technology in the Jungle

Technology is like a piano.
You won't get any music from it unless you play it.

—*Jane Hight McMurry*

Technology is the 21st century gender equalizer. It is the instrument that has revolutionized women's ability to compete at the highest levels by making it easy to do business. The Internet provides women an opportunity to communicate with fewer prejudices and misunderstandings as it is a gender-blind vehicle. Perhaps the Internet's greatest value to women is the access to information it provides without regard to position or status. Access to information is power.

Telephones

The telephone continues to be the most dominant global communication tool for selling, buying, and making lasting impressions. It is also the dominant source of frustration. Disrespected callers on average tell seven to nine people when they have a poor telephone experience.

Making connections over the telephone is a lot like making connections with people face-to-face. Do the same homework and know as much about your telephone conversation partner before you talk on the phone as you would if you were going to meet in person at a networking event. Your verbal impression on the telephone conveys 87% of your education, background, ability, and personality in as little as sixty seconds. Be enthusiastic, confident, and attentive. Small talk is huge talk over the phone. It sets the tone for communication at a distance.

Use the same body language you do speaking over the telephone as you do in person. People can "hear" your smile when you begin with a pleasant greeting. People can also hear when you are eating food, chewing gum, guzzling drinks and multi-tasking on the computer. Be professional and stay focused on the person at the end of the telephone line.

Say hello and immediately give your first and last names to the person you call. Never say, "Guess who this is?" Ask the person you call if it is a good time to talk if your call will last longer than a few minutes. This shows your respect of his time. Tell the person how much of his time you need so he can schedule a time to talk to you if you are going to need more than three to five minutes during your impromptu call. If you tell the person that your call will take five minutes, then do not talk longer than five minutes or you will jeopardize trust. If the person you call says that he only has a specified amount of time, respect his time and limit the length of your call. Time is more precious than money because we can always get more money, but we cannot get more time. Do not rob people of their time or force them to give you more time than you said you would take from them or they have to give you.

Prepare an agenda and speak from notes. That way you won't waste time—yours and others—and you'll appear smart and efficient. Identify your purpose early in the conversation. Anticipate questions and possible objections to avoid additional calls.

Asking for feedback is important because you cannot see the face of your communication partner to make sure that what you are saying is understood. Eliciting feedback by asking, "Do you have any questions/thoughts/suggestions?" will help. Clarify what you hear by saying, "If I understand you correctly..." "So you are saying that..." "This is what I understand you are telling me..."

Take care not to sound abrupt by using phrases like, "Hang on." "Hold on." "Who's calling?" "Speak up!"

Schedule a follow-up conversation and include a time and deadlines. You can do this by saying, "I'll get back to you on..."

If you need something from the other person, be sure to say "please" as in "Would you please...?"

Demonstrate what you have the power to do when someone asks you to do something. Avoid saying that it's not your job and that you cannot help. Better choices are saying, "While I'm not able to...." "I will speak to someone about your concern." "I'll find out..."

The way you close a call creates a lasting impression. State the action you'll take on the business discussed.

For example, "Here's how I can help..." "Here's what needs to be done..."

When you end the call say, "Thank you" and speak in the past tense. For example say, "Thank you, I'm glad we chatted." End with a professional, "Good-bye," not "Bye-bye," "See ya," or "So long."

Answer incoming phone calls by the third ring. Greet the caller in a friendly manner. Protect your time by politely saying at the beginning of the call, "I only have five minutes." Schedule return calls for longer conversations.

Show respect for others who are giving you their time face-to-face by not answering incoming calls when they are in your presence. If you must answer an incoming call, excuse yourself to answer the call and make your conversation brief. Not doing this sends the message that the caller's time is more important to you than the time of the person standing face-to-face.

Your answering machine should have a professional greeting on it that is brief and polite. Be current if your message includes a holiday or an auto responder.

When you leave a voice mail message, say your first and last names. Say your name slowly at the beginning of your message. Spell your name if it is somewhat complicated. Providing your telephone number early in your message saves the listener from having to listen repeatedly to your entire message if he needs to listen a second time for your number. Your message should be brief, not exceeding two minutes. Say please and thank you as you clearly state what you need from the person. Let the listener know the best time to return your call to avoid telephone tag. Don't leave a teaser message like, "Call me. I have something important to tell you."

Cell phones

Your phone should have a professional ring. Turn the ringer off or change to vibrate mode when you carry your phone in public. Using cell phones in public is rude. Excuse yourself from a group if you must talk on a cell phone. The ringing of cell phones and subsequent conversations in restaurants, theatres, etc., is annoying and unprofessional. You send the message that the person on the phone is more important than the people spending time in your presence. The people standing in front of you may tell you they do not mind that you ignore them while you talk on the phone, but you are being rude and insulting them by devaluing their time. Exceptions are for extraordinary situations such as when a person is on a kidney transplant list or has left children with a baby sitter. Even then, monitor calls with caller ID and let voice mail service record messages. Return non-emergency calls later and in private.

Instant Messaging/Texting

Instant messaging/texting is wonderful because... well, it's instant. Be brief. It's not for serious, emotional, or confrontational issues. Be courteous when you use it.

Be aware that you will likely offend those in your presence if you text on your phone in public places and in meetings. Be careful not to appear to place technology ahead of those you are with face-to-face.

When you do text or instant message, check the availability of those you contact. Use "busy" and "away" message features to avoid misunderstandings and to let people know that you are not ignoring them. Use spell/grammar check regardless of the mode used. Emoticons appear unprofessional and rushed so be careful using them.

As a courtesy to your instant messaging/texting partner, summarize attachments and send large quantities of information as attachments instead of copying/ pasting into the message. Courtesy remains important when you text. Use PLS/THX. Be professional at all times.

IM/Texting Shorthand will help keep your messages brief. The following are a few of the most common.

- BFN (bye for now)
- CID (consider it done)
- CU (see you)
- FYI (for your information)
- IOW (in other words)
- L8R (later)
- NRB (need reply by date)
- NRN (no response necessary)
- PLS (please)
- THX (thanks)

- TIA (thanks in advance)
- TY (thank you)
- TBA (to be announced)
- YW (you're welcome)

Twitter

Twitter is for the purpose of answering, "What are you doing?" Twitter is free and much faster than logging into a website content management system to transmit to a large audience. Use it to transmit instantly to inform millions of people about something happening including public safety alerts, real time news alerts, business developments, and soliciting feedback.

Messages called tweets are limited to 140 characters. Think of Twitter as a micro-blog to update your network. The great thing about tweeting is that it humanizes you to a very large group.

You can use Twitter to network, brand, and market to get what you want, need, and deserve. However, use Twitter to promote moderately or you will lose followers. The exception is when you set up a Twitter account named after a product or service for the sole purpose of promoting. In that case, your followers have a different set of expectations.

Twitter Power points

- Clear sender
- Answer direct questions
- Share knowledge/Give value

- Avoid excessive linking
- Retweet good tips and give credit to others
- Be up-to-date on things
- Respect others' privacy
- Don't ask for re-tweets unless broadcasting a question
- Avoid aggressive following to prevent Twitter suspension
- Add small number of interesting people to build your network
- Avoid ghost twittering

Email

Email often causes problems in the workplace because people sloppily dash off words that convey their meaning poorly and thus cause problems. To avoid this, think of email communication like face-to-face communication.

Effective use of email requires that you attend to six elements.

1. *The "To" field.* Check and double check the address you select just like you would take care to call a person by the correct name when you are face-to-face.

2. *The "From" field* should have your full name in proper caps to clearly identify you as the sender.

3. *The "Subject" line.* Avoid using the word "hi" and spam words in your subject line. Change the subject line for your replies. Your subject line

should have 5-7 words that clearly indicate the content of your message. Write attention-getting subjects because 41% of emails are opened according to the subject line! Think of your subject line as a news line in the newspaper that attracts you to read an article.

An example of a weak subject line is a one word subject such as: *Meeting*. A strong subject line for an email about a meeting might be: *Urgent meeting May 20 @ 2 pm in Jungle Room!*

A technique for ease and speed is to simply use the subject line for the entire message. Do so by placing either your initials or the letters EOM (end of message) at the end of your message. Here's a sample of this technique:

Mon doesn't work. How's Wed? —JHM
Wed is NG. How's Th? —EOM
Th is fine. —JHM
See you Th at 3:15 —EOM

4. *The "Greeting"* is like a personal handshake. Don't omit it. Begin with "Hello" or "Dear."

5. *The "Body"* of your email should have correct grammar. Just because it is an instant communication does not mean that it can be sloppy. Create a good feeling by writing sentences that indicate a positive tone such as: "Hope all is well," "Please," "May I," "Great job," "Good thinking," "Congratulations."

- Respect space. Use plenty of white space.

- When you ask for something in an email don't forget to say, "I appreciate your help," or "Thank you in advance."

- Be clear and be sure to give a concrete request/task/time deadline when you ask someone to do something via email.

- Send requests to only one person to avoid diluting responsibility.

- If you really want somebody to do something, CC someone powerful.

- Seek feedback by directly asking for it, as in "Let me know what you're thinking." Verify the recipient's understanding of your message and confirm important time lines.

- Nagging with a repeat email request is okay because if someone has not responded to your email request within 48 hours they probably aren't going to respond. This also applies to telephone message requests.

Email often causes problems because we cannot hear vocal inflection, see facial expressions, or read body language. You can however set the tone with punctuation.

The dash (—) can heighten what's enclosed as if you're raising your voice. For example, The Business Jungle Company—winner of the service award—just introduced its new product line.

Parentheses ( ) can play down what's enclosed as if you're lowering your voice. For example, The Business

Jungle Company (winner of the service award) just introduced its new product line. Commas (,) can neutralize what's enclosed. For example, The Business Jungle Company, winner of the service award, just introduced its new product line. Just as you use gestures in face-to-face communication, you can use **bold**, <u>underscore</u>, and *italic* features to gesture in your email.

Keep your correspondence reader focused. Avoid limp language and jargon. Say what you mean. If you forward an email, tell the recipient why you are forwarding and what's expected. People get annoyed with mail that clogs their inbox and seems forwarded for no apparent reason.

6. *The "Closing"* of your email is like a handshake that you extend at the end of a face-to-face communication. Conclude with "Best regards," "Warm regards," "Sincerely." And finally, write your first and last names.

You can use your signature as powerful passive promotion of your business but keep the basic info to 70 characters—4–6 lines max. You don't need to include everything. Use caps correctly and avoid colors and graphics.

Ten E-Mail Commandments

1. Avoid hasty, error-filled messages.
2. Reply promptly or use a current auto responder.

3. BE CONCISE. Avoid lengthy messages. Do not include earlier material that the people need to scroll down to read. SUMMARIZE!

4. Avoid personal messages not relevant to business, i.e. jokes, inappropriate material.

5. Don't use email to transmit sensitive material or relay bad news.

6. Save email that is business related or personally significant. A record of communication can be valuable.

7. Avoid spamming/mass-emailing commercial material and chain letters.

8. Be careful forwarding e-mails and pressing "reply to all."

9. Avoid flaming and shouting (all caps).

10. Avoid sending attached files to people who may not have the necessary software to decode them or whose inbox may have a small size limit.

Facebook

Be careful what you post on Facebook. Employers frequently look at employees' public profiles to determine the suitability of job candidates as well as to learn information about current employees. Post public photos that reflect you as a professional. Be careful not to offer TMI (too much information) on your Facebook page. Friend and defriend people carefully. Use the appropriate privacy setting. Create a limited profile. Keep a friendly tone by avoiding ALL CAPS and sarcasm.

LinkedIn

LinkedIn is a business-oriented social networking site predominantly used for professional networking. It has more than 100 million registered global users. Use it to maintain a list of contact details of people with whom you have a professional connection.

LinkedIn can help you get what you want, need, and deserve in a number of ways. First, it can help you connect with people you know and to people your connections know. You can gain an introduction to others through a mutual contact. LinkedIn is a terrific tool demonstrating the power of weak connections. Very few people who get jobs actually know the person who hires them. People most likely get jobs because somebody recommended them. The person recommending is not necessarily best friends with the person who hires, but there is a connection. LinkedIn helps you identify connections who can link you to others.

You can use LinkedIn to find jobs, people, and business opportunities. You can review the profile of potential employers and determine which of your contacts can introduce you to a potential employer or connection you want to know. Posted photos on LinkedIn help to identify you and help you identify others.

According to LinkedIn research, people with more than twenty connections on LinkedIn are thirty-four more times likely to be approached with a job opportunity than people with less than five.

Use LinkedIn to increase your visibility. People do business with people they know. Adding connections on LinkedIn increases the chance that people searching for a person with your skill set will find and choose you.

Include a link to your LinkedIn profile as part of your email signature. This is a tasteful and appropriate way to let people see your credentials.

Use LinkedIn to prepare for conversation. Read about those you'll meet at an event, interview with for a job, or approach to sell a product, service, or idea.

Chapter Thirteen

When Things Go Bump in the Night: Dealing with Uncomfortable Situations and Living to Talk about It!

To succeed in life, you need three things:
a wishbone, a backbone and a funnybone.

—*Reba McEntire*

My mother and mentor, Joan Williams Hight, was a fun-loving, fearless lioness who loved life and enjoyed learning and trying new things. She didn't waste time on what she didn't like doing or find necessary. Once she tried baking biscuits and afterwards said she wouldn't spend any more time baking biscuits because she didn't like baking biscuits and she could buy ready-made ones that were less expensive and better than hers. She tried almost everything except bungee jumping, traveled as much of the world as she could, and could talk to just about anyone about anything.

Needlepoint was one of the things she learned in order to understand the hobby of many of her friends. She chose to invest time creating only two needlepoint pieces. The first was a small needlepoint square she framed. It has a grinning frog hanging onto the knot at the end of a rope. She stitched under the frog,

"When you're at the end of your rope, tie a knot and hang on."

Many days you'll find yourself at the end of a knot in the jungle because conflict is an expected part of life in the jungle. Plan ahead. Foresee confrontations. Be on guard. Prepare to respond to danger so you can hang on to the strong knot you've made in order to reach your goals. And most importantly, *keep a sense of humor.*

Powerful and polite women have gentle souls but tough hides. They are admired. They are respected. They are loved by many—but not liked by all. They do not suffer from the disease to please.

The reasons people do not like you may be because they are jealous of your accomplishments, you remind them of someone they don't like, you are prettier than they are, you are richer than they are, you are more talented than they are, etc. You will never be able to please everyone no matter how hard you try, so there is no need to try. Remain honest. Do what is right and focus on what is best for your life. The bottom line is that success and power are not the result of a popularity contest.

A lot of people wouldn't give Stefani Joanne Angelina Germanotta, better known as Lady Gaga, the time of day when she began her career. In an interview with Jocelyn Vena for *MTV News,* Lady Gaga said, "Some people didn't get it. Some people still don't get it. I read reviews sometimes and I'm like, 'Wow, that guy really doesn't f---ing like me.' Like, they really don't get it, but that's cool." Lady Gaga elaborated that before her songs became radio staples, she was hard-pressed to convince anyone to play them on the radio. "The real struggle is that they didn't want to play my music on the radio. We fought and we fought and I played every club. I had chicken dinner with every program director I could get my hands on."

Lady Gaga now towers over the pop culture landscape with success getting what *Gaga* wants, needs, and deserves. Her success is due to more than talent... nothing is more common than unsuccessful musicians with only talent unless it is unsuccessful men and women with only education. Her success is due to a combination of talent, a crystal clear vision for what she wants, persistent action on her plan to reach identified goals, and doing what is right for her even though everyone does not like her music and style. Another pop culture idol from a previous generation, Ricky Nelson, intoned the same guiding principle that rewarded him with the same top of the charts success that Lady Gaga enjoys. In his famous song "Garden Party" Nelson croons, "You can't please everyone so you gotta please yourself." No matter what type of jungle you choose to navigate to get what *you* want need and deserve, you must have: a clear vision of what you want; a goal; skills to reach your goal; a plan with steps to reach your goal; persistent action on your plan; and the courage to do what is right for you.

Keep a good sense of humor as you begin to get what you want and if someone calls you a bitch remember that it's a compliment because you are a **B**abe **I**n **T**otal **C**ontrol of **H**erself.

Deal with problems honestly and immediately. The truth always comes out—if not immediately it will eventually. The winds of gossip will magnify the problem the longer you wait to tell the truth and accept responsibility. Taking immediate ownership will help you retain control over the problem and diffuse the energy of your detractors. After all, you will have said everything including that you are sorry, so there is nothing else that detractors can add. If you don't accept ownership early, the problem is guaranteed to fester, diffusing you of power and causing you to lose control of the problem. Take responsibility for your actions when you make a mistake without making excuses. Avoid rationalizing aloud, offering explanations, or making excuses for your errors. People in the corporate jungle really do not care why you screw up—they just want you to correct the problem. In addition, making excuses sets you up for criticism.

Apologize and do whatever you can to make amends and then do one thing more. Doing what is expected plus adding one thing more that is unexpected will set you apart.

The difference between winners and losers, the powerful and the powerless, is not ability. It is how they respond to the mistakes they make. Powerful people have an unfailing resolve to pick themselves up after their mistakes, fix what they can fix, and keep right on going to reach their goals. That's what you must do if you want to win and have power. Get up, get out of bed, put one foot in front of the other. Fall down seven times...stand up eight!

Power comes from a positive attitude. Stephen Covey's 90/10 Principle is true. He says that we have no control over ten percent of what happens to us in life, but we determine the other 90 percent. Your response, your reaction, the 90 percent is what will determine your success. Your success will result from your work and your attitude.

Don't take yourself too seriously. Laugh at yourself. You are responsible for your happiness. Take control of your attitude the minute you wake. The first thing I do is to give thanks for my blessings and to ask for strength to fully live the new day. Then I literally ROAR out loud. Roaring makes me laugh out loud—*at myself*. Starting the day with gratitude and remembering that help is present every day encourages a positive attitude to meet the day's challenges. The laughter that erupts after roaring reminds me not to take myself too seriously as a human being who is by nature going to make mistakes. Try roaring when you wake up. You have to open your mouth wide to suck in air and then exercise your vocal cords to do this. I'm willing to bet you'll laugh at yourself.

My sports broadcast journalist daughter, Win, made a well-publicized tongue slip on national television on one of her routine updates for Golf Channel. The tongue slip was regarding Tiger Wood's withdrawal from one of his first golf tournaments after taking time off due to his widely reported indiscretions and marital woes. Win meant to report that the reason for Tiger's withdrawal was due to "a bulging 'disc' in his neck," but instead her tongue substituted a "ck" sound for an "sc" sound. She immediately corrected her error on-air and continued with her report. Win called home as soon as she was off the air.

I told her, "You are human and made a mistake like all humans, and you will make more. You have to laugh at yourself when you do something like this." She started laughing and soon we were both *roaring!*

Win's next update was in nineteen minutes. She went back on air and continued—this time flawlessly.

She laughed and it seemed that people all over the world laughed with her. Friends living in Canada and friends traveling in Barcelona heard it on the BBC. For several days her name and tongue slip were among the most googled in the world. Even though she had made a tongue slip, her ability to be a good sport, to laugh at herself, and to continue her work without skipping a beat won her praise from colleagues, friends, and acquaintances.

Not all things can be laughed off but when they can, laughter truly is the best way to address what cannot be changed. Laugh at yourself.

Forgive others when they make mistakes.

Act immediately when it is up to you to deal with the serious mistakes of others. Taking action quickly and with integrity is important. You'll find that if you do not beat around the bush to get to the heart of the problem and honestly address the situation in a professional manner that you'll retain the power and authority you've worked to achieve. Always do what is right even if it is painful to people you like.

Disagreements will occur. Pick your battles but do not run from confrontation when you have a problem that needs to be addressed. Letting problems fester will increase your anxiety. Deal with problems and move on.

Powerful people are in control of their emotions. Women who raise their voices are perceived as disagreeable hotheads so instead of raising your voice when you are angry, respond with powerful and descriptive language expressing the actual reason for your anger. People can tell who is losing an argument by observing who is yelling loudest. You'll look like a loser if you lose your temper and yell.

Tears will lessen your power. If you become angry or tearful, remove yourself from the situation until you've regained composure. Say something brief such as, "Excuse me. I'll be back in a few minutes." If you need more time, say, "This is not a good time for me to talk. Let's discuss this later."

Housework, if you do it right, will kill you.

—*Erma Bombeck*

Chapter Fourteen

The Lioness Sleeps Tonight: Recharging and Renewal

If you neglect to recharge a battery, it dies.
And if you run full speed ahead without stopping for water,
you lose momentum to finish the race.

—*Oprah Winfrey*

It's a jungle out there. You must recharge for the hunt. Instead of trying to do it all, choose what to do, when to do it, and do it well. As women, we often try to prove our worth by taking on responsibilities that keep us from reaching our goals. There is never time for recharging and renewal, so you need to make the time. Determine your priorities. Set your goals. Finding time to recharge and renew is possible with time management.

Time robbers will steal your time if you do not know what they are and do not take steps to stop them. You must manage your time if you want to find time to recharge and renew. Consider the following time thieves and power robbers.

- Inability to say "no"
- Lack of planning/focus
- Lack of clear goals/responsibilities

- Unexpected issues
- Lack of control/shuffling through piles
- Poor physical setup
- Too many meetings
- Unnecessary meetings
- Disorganization/clutter
- Not delegating
- Poor networking
- Unreasonable expectations
- Perfectionism
- Procrastination
- Poor planning
- Lack of boundaries setting
- Interruptions/unscheduled meetings
- Urgency addiction
- Bad attitude
- Negative people

Interruptions are one of the greatest undetected time robbers. It takes time to get back on track. *Time* magazine cited in an article on time that Basix, Inc, an information technology research firm, determined from a study of 1,000 office workers from top management on down that the cost of time lost due to interruptions averages 2.1 hours per day, or 28% of the workday.

Researchers from the University of California at Anaheim found that office workers devote only eleven minutes per task before being interrupted by the sound of an email, a telephone call, or someone physically entering the work area. Most significantly, their research revealed that it takes an average of twenty-five minutes to return to focus on an original task.

Do not be a slave to people who interrupt you with telephone calls. It is your choice to answer, so don't feel that you must answer a call the instant your telephone rings. Use caller ID and let your message system take a message for you so you can return calls when it is *convenient for you.* The same goes for the ping of voice mail and text messages. Silence the ping so the sound won't distract you. The following are tips to minimize time lost due to telephone interruptions.

- Stand during telephone calls
- Keep calls short—begin the call with a friendly greeting and tell the person you only have five minutes
- When you place a call, start by announcing the goals for the call
- Don't put your feet up
- Have something in view that you're waiting to get to next
- Return calls early or late in the day to be sure you get through
- Block out times for calls and batch process (do similar things in a series—return calls, emails, etc., at a scheduled time)

Politely manage your time in the office when people walk into your office. Make your office comfortable for you and optionally comfortable for visitors. Consider chairs without cushions or folding chairs so visitors will not stay long. Use the phrases and techniques below to help cut conversations short when people come into your office and you are busy.

- "I'm in the middle of something now."
- "I only have five minutes." (You can always extend this.)
- Stand up, stroll to the door, and thank the person for coming while shaking the person's hand.

Learn to say no. Powerful women know how to manage their lives so they can achieve their goals. The following are powerfully polite ways to say no.

- "Thank you for asking. You deserve the best. Unfortunately, I don't have time to do the job your project deserves. I appreciate you thinking of me."
- "Thank you for asking. I have made so many commitments to others; it would be unfair to them and to you if I took on anything more at this point."
- "Before I take this over from you, what do you think we ought to do about it?"
- "I would like to help you out on this but I don't have the resources available to do the right job for you."

- "Now that's the type of thing I would love to help you with if only I had the time."

- "Just like you, I get overloaded sometimes and have to tell some very special people, 'No.' This is one of those times."

And as you speak, smile!

- "I'm sorry. That's not a priority for me right now."

- "I can't help you on this now, but I can get to it next week. Would that be okay?"

- "I have so much on my plate now I don't know when I can get to it. But I do know someone who can help you now."

- "Before I take this on for you, let me show you a few things so that you might be able to do it yourself."

- "If I can't give you a ride to _____ on Friday, how else could you get there safely?"

- "I don't know how soon I can help you on this, but I will get back to you as soon as I am free to help you."

- "I'm sure we're close enough that when I say no you'll understand it's for a good reason."

- "Sure I can help you with your request as long as we both agree and understand that the item I agreed to do for you yesterday is going to have to wait."

Identify people in your network who can help you accomplish your goals and identify people who have the strengths you lack. Network your way to gain power. Target people with skills you need. Help others first get what they need. Remember, "To have a friend, be a friend." What goes around comes around. If you freely give to others first, others will give to you what you need and want.

No one can do everything well. Choose what you are good at and spend your time where you can excel and reach your goals. Delegate tasks that you're not good at or are simple or trivial to others. Delegating can provide you with the time you need to do what is important *to you*. Get a gopher when it comes to simple tasks like running errands, mowing the lawn, and getting gas in your car.

Treat well the people who help you and thank them for their help. Give concrete goals, deadlines, and consequences. Remember, you are more likely to get what you want when you make it clear what it is you want.

Procrastination is the thief of time and power. Weak people procrastinate because they are afraid of rejection, failure, fear that they will create more problems than they will solve, or because they have distaste for a task. Powerful women have a spine and like the Nike ad says, they "just do it."

Women who get what they want, need, and deserve are organized. They don't spend time looking for things or running out of supplies. If you go into the workspace of a powerful woman you will likely find she has a good file system.

Work with a clean work environment. It's true, "Out of sight, out of mind." The reverse is true too! "In sight, in mind" distracts and draws us to "quick" and "fun" things while important tasks are left undone. Work with a clean desk and work environment to facilitate focus. Your habits will inspire others around you. The more you empower others the more power you will have at your fingertips!

A positive attitude will increase your ability to achieve the results you desire. "Fish rots from the head down." If you display a negative attitude, if you are angry, frustrated, anxious, overwhelmed, etc., you will send out vibes that negatively infect those around you. If those who support you in your quest for career success do not have a positive attitude, your progress and power will be impeded. People who are not supportive of your goals, who do not believe in you, who belittle your dreams and goals and give reasons why you will not succeed will hold you down. Stay away from stinking thinking if you want to get what you want, need, and deserve. Let YOUR thoughts and YOUR actions control YOUR destiny.

A quote by Thomas Henry Huxley (1825-95), English biologist and writer, is on my desk as a reminder to do what needs to be done when it needs to be done. "Perhaps the most valuable result of all education is the ability to make yourself do the thing you have to do, when it ought to be done, whether you like it or not; it is the first lesson that ought to be learned; and however early a man's training begins, it is probably the last lesson that he learns thoroughly."

Advice from a Sanskrit text is as valuable today as it was centuries ago. "Whenever there is a decision to be made, make it as wisely as possible and forget it for the moment of absolute truth may never arise." Remember these words of wisdom in every aspect of your life. Don't even waste time hemming and hawing over what to order in a restaurant when you could be enjoying the company of your dinner partners. If you don't know what to order, ask your waiter for advice or narrow your choice and then let your waiter choose. The goal you want is good food and for it to satisfy you. Most day-to-day decisions are not life or death decisions. Taking too much time to make unimportant decisions will rob you of precious time you can choose to spend on what you value.

Do the hardest, most important, and dreaded tasks first so you can focus on what you want to do.

Manage your time and find balance in your life by using the 80/20 rule of time management known as the Pareto Principle. The Pareto Principle is the result of a finding by Italian economist Vilfredo Pareto in 1897. Pareto observed that 20% of a person's efforts produce 80% of the results.

Simply put, the 80/20 rule states that the relationship between input and output is rarely, if ever, balanced. When applied to work, it means that approximately 20% of your efforts produce 80% of the results. Learning to recognize and then focus on that 20% is the key to making the most effective use of your time. Here are two quick tips to develop powerful 80/20 thinking.

Take a good look at the people around you. Twenty percent of the people in your life probably give you 80 percent of the support and satisfaction you need. They are your true advocates. Take good care of them. You can probably name several friends and family members who would be there for you under any circumstances. Do not place them on your back burner.

Examine your work. Ask yourself, "What do I really want to do with my life and my time? What 20% of my work should I be focusing on?"

Even if you're skeptical, follow the 80/20 principle for a few days just to see what happens. You can start by immediately implementing the following 20% suggestions.

Read less. Identify the 20% of the reading material you have and determine what is most valuable. Read the most valuable and trash the rest.

Keep current. Make yourself aware of new technological innovations and use what saves you the most time.

Remember the basics. As you increase your power and grow your career, remember your ethics and values. Let them guide your decision-making and you are bound to end up focusing on the right 20 percent.

Walt Disney said, "If you can dream it, you can do it." Disney World was built in 366 days from the first shovel to the first ticket sold! Only 5% of people set goals even though according to Franklin Covey people who set goals and write them down have a 95% greater chance of attaining goals than people who do not. Write down your goal. Write down the steps to reach your goal and a time line for accomplishing your goal. A faint pen is more powerful than the keenest mind. Put your goal in writing.

Determine a specific deadline to reach your goal. Cyril Northcote Parkinson coined what is known as Parkinson's Law, "Work expands so as to fill the time available for its completion." Deadlines are vital. NOW spelled backwards is WON.

You can change a plan—but only when you have one! You've probably heard before that "if you fail to plan, you plan to fail." If you want to get what you want, need, and deserve, you must plan to have it.

Schedule time for yourself. You don't find time for important things—you make it. Perfection on most things except things like neurosurgery is unnecessary, so give yourself permission to relax. Most things in life are pass/fail. Seriously now, you don't have to iron sheets to get a good night's sleep. You don't have to slave over a hot stove and set a table with fine china to entertain your friends. It's okay to order take-out and to have a little dust on your furniture. Being a perfectionist at things that are not vital is a waste of important time. People will appreciate that you value them and will be grateful for your gesture of hospitality. If they do not, they are not worth your time.

Respect the time of others just as you respect your own time. Show up on time. Do what you say you will do when you say you will do it. If you don't, you will likely never get what you want, need, and deserve. People know you by the actions that back up your words. If your actions do not back up your words, people will not want to invest their time to act on your behalf to help you get what you want and need because they will feel you do not deserve their time and effort.

Now that you know how to find time, take time to renew. Seventy-five percent of all doctor visits are for stress-related illnesses such as headaches, stomach-aches, insomnia and fatigue. Looking after yourself is not selfish. If you don't look after yourself you will be unable to look after your career and the people you love. Eat a balanced diet, exercise, and get the rest you need. It's vital to your power. Do this every day and don't feel guilty about it. The world's problems are not yours to solve. Don't fool yourself or let others fool you into thinking that they are. Make time to do things you will reminisce about when you are an old lioness. Is the project that seems so urgent to complete today more important in the scheme of life than the time you could spend hiking with a loved one in the park, visiting a friend, or savoring a sunset? Consider what you want to leave as your legacy. Is it money or is it something more precious?

You are responsible for your life and for your happiness. Notice the good things in life even when sad things, maddening things, inevitably occur. Laugh often and laugh at yourself. Take control of your attitude the minute you wake.

Feeling good inside won't last throughout your day if you just think about yourself and your own happiness. I learned a lot about happiness by observing my mom, the wisest happiest lioness I've ever known. She roared a lot. A lot of the time she roared for people who couldn't roar for themselves. She traveled to the NC General Assembly to roar for ERA women's rights in the 1960s. She was the first director of the regional mental health clinic in her hometown where she roared for mentally challenged people. As she aged, she realized the needs of the elderly and roared as she directed the establishment of the first senior center in my hometown where at the time she and her program for the aging were nationally recognized for feeding more elderly people the best food for less money than anywhere in the United States. She was always thinking about other people and doing for others without expecting anything in return. She was happy.

If you stop for a moment and you think about your happiest time, you'll probably realize the same two things I observed about my mom when she seemed happiest and most motivated. One, you weren't thinking about yourself. Two, you were giving or sharing with someone else. If you want to be happy, forget about yourself, give and share.

My daughters were in first and third grades when my mother and I traveled with them to France. We toured castles, cathedrals, and famous monuments including the beaches of Normandy where rows of white crosses mark the graves of thousands of people who lived roaring for what they believed in.

On our final night in France, my mom was determined that we go to the Folies Bergere in Paris. When she learned it was closed, she decided we would go to the Moulin Rouge. I was opposed, saying that the girls were too young, but mom was unrelenting and said that it was a part of Paris the girls should not miss. I reluctantly agreed to let them attend.

Our front-row table included a cooler of French champagne. I stopped the waiter when he began to pour champagne for my daughters but my mother said, "Let them have a little. One day they will say they had their first sip of champagne with their grandmother in Paris." When the glasses were poured, mom raised her glass to toast us and to toast life and the freedom to live it fully and well.

Twenty years later when my daughter, Win, was asked in an interview if she could go back in time to have a conversation with anyone who'd ever lived, she said, "Big Joan, my grandmother." When asked why she chose her grandmother she said, "Because she was fun to be with, could talk about anything, was curious about everything, and she cared about me and other people. She always knew what to do and how to do it and she had fun doing it."

I mentioned earlier that my mom chose time to needlepoint only two things in her life. One was the framed smiling frog and the other was a happy monkey swinging through the jungle. She placed the needlepoint of the happy monkey on the cushion of a hard bentwood chair. I'm sure it was her way of reminding those who would see her joyful monkey on the chair made for rest that like her monkey, they too should pause to rest and not take the jungle so seriously that they'd miss the fun of journeying through it.

As a woman, you need to be secure in the fact that the productive happy life you want is the result of more than hard honest work and skill. It is the result of a balanced life. To achieve that balance you must take time to relax as well as take time to enjoy swinging through life with the rest of creation. It's not only important, it is OKAY for you to pause for five minutes in the day to stop taking care of things, to stop being clever, important, efficient, imaginative, the perfect career woman, girlfriend, wife, or mother. If it's been a long time since you've stopped to rest and play—*risk it*. Hang on to the rope, open your eyes, pull back your lips, show your gums, throw your head back and enjoy life just for the sheer joy of the gift of life!

When I delivered my first daughter, Win, I was overwhelmed with emotion and suddenly realized all the time my mom had given to me providing me with learning opportunities and teaching me by example. My eyes filled with tears as I held my newborn daughter. I looked at my mother and said, "Mom, I can never thank you enough for all you've done for me and for all the time you've given me."

She smiled a smile that made her nose crinkle and said, "Having a daughter is a great gift. Giving and doing for you has given me pleasure. Live, learn, laugh, and pass it on."

When I had my second daughter, Allison, mom's eyes twinkled and her nose crinkled again. This time she said, "The only thing more wonderful than one daughter is two!"

Thank you for taking the time to read this book and for giving me the opportunity to "pass it on." Live, learn, laugh, pass it on, and ROAR to get what you want, need, and deserve!

END

BIBLIOGRAPHY

Adler, Ronald B. and George Rodman. *Understanding Human Communication.* Fortworth, Texas: Holt, Rinehart and Winston, Inc., 1991.

Ailes, Roger. *You Are The Message.* New York: Doubleday, 1998.

Allesandra, Tony. *Charisma.* New York: Time Warner, 1998.

Bahr, Candace. *It's More Than Money – It's Your Life: The New Money Club for Women.* New Jersey: John Wiley & Sons, Inc., 2003.

Beckwith, Harry. *Selling the Invisible.* New York: Warner Books, 1997.

Bick, Julie. *All I Really Need To Know In Business I Learned At Microsoft.* New York: Pocket Books, 1997.

Bixler, Susan and Lisa Scherrer. *Take Action!* New York: Ballantine Books, 1996.

Bolton, Robert. *People Skills.* New York: Simon & Schuster, 1979.

Bolton, Robert and Dorothy Grover Bolton. *People Styles at Work.* New York: American Management Association, 1996.

Bowman, Daria Price and Maureen LaMarca. *Writing Notes With A Personal Touch.* New York; Michael Friedman Publishing Group, 1998.

Boyett, Joseph H. and Henry P. Conn. *Workplace 2000: The Revolution Reshaping American Business.* New York: Penguin Books, 1991.

Brown, Charles T. and Charles Van Riper. *Speech and Man.* Englewood Cliffs, New Jersey: Prentice-Hall, Inc., 1966.

Brown, Steve. *How To Talk So People Will Listen.* Grand Rapids: Baker Publishing Company, 1993.

Catalystwomen.org, *Women in Corporate Leadership: Progress and Prospects,* 1999.

Dale, Paulette. *Did You Say Something Susan?* New York: Kensington Publishing Corporation, 1999.

Decker, Bert. *The Art of Communicating.* Menlo Park: Crisp Publications, 1988.

Dimitrius, Jo-Ellen and Mark Mazzarella. *Reading People.* New York: Random House, 1998.

Donaldson, Les. *Conversational Magic.* Paramus, New Jersey: Prentice Hall, 1981.

Drobot, Eve. *Class Acts.* New York: VanNostrand Reinhold Company, 1982.

Feldhahn, Shaunti. *"The Male Factor: The Unwritten Rules, Misperceptions, and Secret Beliefs of Men in the Workplace."* New York: Crown Publishers, 2009.

Fountain, Elizabeth Haas. *The Polished Professional.* Hawthorne, New Jersey: Career Press, 1994.

Frank, Milo. *How to Get Your Point Across in 30 Seconds or Less.* New York: Simon and Schuster, 1986.

Frankel, Lois P. *Nice Girls Don't Get the Corner Office.* New York: Hatchette Book Group, 2004.

Gabor, Don. *Talking with Confidence for the Painfully Shy.* New York: Crown Trade Paperbacks, 1997.

Glass, Lillian. *Say It Right: How to Talk in Any Social or Business Situation.* New York: Perigee Books, 1992.

Griffin, Jack. *How to Say It Best.* Paramus, New Jersey: Prentice Hall, 1994.

Hall, Edward T. *The Silent Language.* New York: Doubleday, 1981.

Hoff, Ron. *Do Not Go Naked into Your Next Presentation.* Kansas City: Andrews and McMeel, 1997.

Hybels, Saundra and Richard L. Weaver, II. *Communicating Effectively.* New York: Random House, 1989.

Jones, Charles. *What Makes Winners Win.* Secaucus, New Jersey: Carol Publishing Group, 1998.

Katz, Donald. *Just Do It.* Holbrook, Massachusetts: Adams Media Corporation, 1994.

Kramer, Marc. *Power Networking.* Chicago, Illinois: VGM Career Horizons, 1997.

Lavington, Camille. *You've Only Got Three Seconds.* New York: Doubleday, 1997.

Leeds, Dorothy. *Smart Questions: A New Strategy for Successful Managers.* New York: McGraw-Hill, 1987.

Lowndes, Leil. *How to Be a People Magnet.* Chicago: Contemporary Books, 2001.

Martinet, Jeanne. *The Art of Mingling.* New York: Thorsons, 1992.

McMurry, Jane Hight. *The Dance Steps of Life.* USA: Stellar Publishing, 2001.

McMurry, Jane Hight. *The Etiquette Advantage.* USA: Stellar Publishing, 2002.

Michelli, Dena and Alison Straw. *Successful Networking.* Hong Kong: Barron's, 1997.

Mindell, Phyllis. *A Woman's Guide to the Language of Success.* Paramus, New Jersey: Prentice Hall, 1995.

Molloy, John T. *New Women's Dress for Success.* New York: Warner Books, Inc. 1996.

Myers, Marc. *How To Make Luck.* Los Angeles: Renaissance Books, 1999.

Pausch, Randy. *The Last Lecture.* New York: Hyperion, 2008.

Peacher, Georgiana. *Speak To Win.* New York: Bell Publishing Company, 1985.

Salmansohn, Karen. *How To Succeed in Business Without a Penis.* New York: Three Rivers Press, 1996.

Slovic, Susan Wilson. *The Girls' Guide to Power & Success.* New York: MFJ Books, 2001.

Tannen, Deborah. *Talking From 9 To 5.* New York: William Morrow and Company, Inc., 1994.

Westmoreland, Rose. *Building Self-Esteem.* Torrance, California: Frank Schaffer Publication, Inc., 1994.

Williams, Jennifer. *Staying In Touch.* New York: Hearst Books, 1998.

Young, Lauren. Businessweek.com: *The Motherhood Penalty: Working Moms Face Pay Gap Vs. Childless Peers,* 2009.

INDEX

180   JANE HIGHT MCMURRY

About the Author

Jane Hight McMurry is president of Effective Business Communication, a popular professional speaker, the author of several books, and taught at the University of North Carolina-Chapel Hill and UNC-Wilmington. Her interest in communication that gets results began while she was a student at Oxford University in England. Her knowledge and understanding of communication differences and English resulted in a college president's hiring her to found the first English as a Second Language program in the Research Triangle Park of North Carolina.

McMurry is an internationally recognized communication skills expert quoted in print and broadcast media. Her Socially Smart® tips were broadcast throughout The People's Republic of China as the Chinese prepared to host the 2008 Olympic Games and continue to achieve leadership in the global market.

Visit the author at janemcmurry.com or in the jungle at navigatingthelipstickjungle.com for information about having the author speak to your organization or group. For additional and bulk copies of this book, please email the publisher at publisher@stellar-publishing.com

Ask Questions. Get Answers.

Visit the heart of the jungle!

www.NavigatingTheLipstickJungle.com

CPSIA information can be obtained at www.ICGtesting.com
Printed in the USA
LVOW081205290412

279584LV00001B/119/P